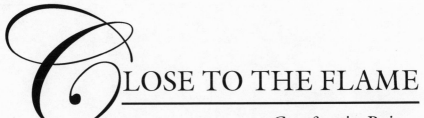

CLOSE TO THE FLAME

Comfort in Pain—
the Memory of Love and a Well-Lived Emptiness

S. C. Rackes

To order additional copies of this book, contact:
Xlibris Corporation
1-888-795-4274
www.Xlibris.com
Orders@Xlibris.com

For my Yosef and especially for my daughter,
Stacy Carol. Also for GM and Don, a love that
lasted and continues forever and ever.

This book is written in memory of a real love as told to the author. It is one of the greatest loves I have ever known. To those who lived and who loved. It is a tribute I give to them that honored their vows and walked away with nothing but the memories and, in the end, died alone but still with the love deep inside.

To
Welch and Alma Crawford (my parents) and grandparents

*All paintings are from the author's collection
by artist Glenda Sweitzer.*

Tennessee
December 30, 1993

There are times to heed the inner warnings,
no matter what the world shall say.

"Today is"—the doctor flipped through the pages on his desk calendar—"December 30." "I know what day it is, Rob." Gabriella Franks, fifty-one and still holding, sighed and waited for the lecture she knew was coming. *Dear Lord, I know what day it is,* she thought. *This day has haunted me for seventeen years.*

"I want you in the hospital no later than Sunday afternoon at two." The doctor in his immaculate white coat looked over the top of his silly little half-glasses and gave her a stern look. "That's Sunday, January 2nd, Gabby. Period."

"Too soon," she replied.

He made a steeple of his hands and leaned his chin into them. "Why is that?"

"I have to tell Theo, talk to him. Explain."

Dr. Schraeder shook his gray head. Gabby knew him all too well to know it was an exasperated shake. He was losing his patience with her and with good reason.

"Do you want to tell me why we kept these tests a secret from Theo in the first place?" She tried to give the comment a dismissive laugh.

"We didn't."

"Don't lie to me, Gabby. You're not very good at it."

You're wrong, she thought. *I'm an expert. My whole life has been a lie since 1976.*

Without so much as a breath, the doctor continued. "You scheduled them for when you knew he was out of town. You called Elaine and begged off from our Christmas party so I wouldn't let anything slip, and now, you want an extension of time so you can put off telling him." The intensity of the doctor's stare combined with the truth in his words made Gabby look away.

He's right, of course, she thought. *I hate giving Theo bad news. It upsets his world. Besides, I need to get through this damnable day and night, this damnable anniversary, before I can deal with anything else, even this.*

"Come back, Gabby," the doctor said, his voice softening. "Look at me, where are you right now?"

She did, but it was with a mixture of reluctance and resignation. The dark-paneled room, with its mahogany desk, its crowded bookcases, its many citations and diplomas adorning the walls, was closing in on her. She could feel the walls pulsating, choking the breath out of her.

"Listen carefully, Gabby, your time has run out. You put this surgery off for three years. Now, it's an emergency. That mitral valve has to be replaced now. No more time, no more excuses." Dr. Schraeder studied her quietly for a few minutes. "You will die without it. Is that clear enough for you?" She was looking out the window again. "Weather's getting worse," she said quietly.

It was the doctor's turn to sigh. "I've given up trying to talk to you. I'm scheduling you for surgery at seven thirty, Monday morning. The hospital will expect you no later than two o'clock, Sunday afternoon. You do what you have to do to be there."

I always have, she thought, riding down in the elevator in the ultramodern Medical Arts building, *done what I have to do. Good old Gabby, fantastic Gabby, you are always the best.*

Not only was the day gray and overcast, but also, the winds were whipping up across the parking lot in a late December frenzy. Gabby paused under the portico, made sure she had her car located amid the sea of parked vehicles, then started toward it.

Once she was tucked safely inside, with the raw wind beating against the windows, she simply sat there, huddled against the chill, watching the other people, mostly patients like her, scurry across the lot.

"Stop this," she finally said. "You've got things to do." Mentally berating herself for her lapse into what was awfully close to depression, Gabby turned the key in the ignition, and the Volvo roared to life. Deftly, she backed out of the parking space, followed the lanes to the exit, then took the turn that would lead her to the freeway and home.

The rain started after she took the I-40 split. With each revolution of her tires, each mile she traveled, each *swoosh-clack* of the windshield wipers, the weather worsened. The cascading rain blew across the freeway. A gust of wind shook the Volvo as a sixteen-wheeler sped past. Gabby flicked the windshield wipers to high as the truck's rooster tails of water spewed over her hood and spattered against the windshield, obscuring her vision.

With the semi disappearing rapidly from sight on its plunge southward toward Chattanooga, Gabby slowed down and took her exit off Interstate 75. Driving down the narrow two-lane highway she exited on, she saw the fog cascading down the Smoky Mountains. Mercilessly it engulfed the small town she and Theo called home.

Gabby made a right on Main Street, traveled past the drugstore, the small jewelers, and the florist, then made a left onto Maple Drive. The heavy canopy of trees lining the street drooped under the weight of the rain, and a premature dusk cloaked the well-to-do, well-kept neighborhood she drove through.

"Wonderful," Gabby muttered, turning left again and pulling into the garage behind their old Victorian house. "This will help a whole lot. Depressing weather for a depressing day."

Gabby gathered up her things and made a dash for the house. Annie, their harlequin Great Dane, was the only one to greet her, as she pushed the door open.

"It was terrible, Annie," she said, working her way around the wagging dog into the kitchen. "I have no reprieves left."

Gabby shrugged out of her coat, hung it on the antique coat tree, and went upstairs to change out of her Harvé Benard pantsuit and into her faded jeans. She had things to do.

Theo would be late tonight. He had to fly back from Chicago and his latest business trip. It gave her a perfect time to head into her studio and put the finishing touches on the painting she was doing for her youngest daughter Sam's new apartment.

Gabby knew from experience she had to keep herself busy when this day rolled around each year. If she permitted herself to start her grieving too early, it got out of hand, became more than she could deal with. *Damn it all. Damn you, Graham,* she thought, going downstairs again and heading into the studio she so loved. *Damn me. Damn the world. Why can't I get over you? Leave the past, leave it where I saw you last, in the past, where it belongs? Why do I put myself through this every year?*

The studio was hushed and cozy when Gabby turned the working lights on and flooded the place with light. Sam's painting sat waiting on a huge drafting table under the north-facing bay windows. Gabby turned the radio on then set about her business.

Refusing to let herself think about anything but the work at hand, she didn't even notice the big dog sneak in, turn herself around three times, then settle on the rug behind her.

Her resolve and her work carried her through most of the long afternoon. The rain pelted her windows, but she barely noticed. She was lost in the preliminary sketch of a painting of a field of tulips her youngest daughter had requested. The final painting would have a shadow here, a highlight there, and slowly, there would be a riot of flowers that would come to life under Gab's brushes. She had studied art in college and loved it. It was the one thing that could take her away into another place and time.

The radio in the studio was turned low, so low, only a brief break in her concentration kept her from missing the weather warning completely. Reluctantly she turned back into the demands of the world; she dried her brushes, sat down behind her desk, and then turned the volume up.

"Rain turning to sleet this afternoon, becoming snow by nightfall," the bored announcer said. "Higher elevations are already reporting accumulations of two to three inches." For the first time in hours, Gabby glanced out her windows. To her surprise, the day was dark and threatening. The fog swirled around the backyard and wove a ghostly pattern through the dense foliage growing there. Gabby could barely make out the ivy-covered brick wall separating their property from the house behind them. Here, close to the mountains, the rain was already hitting the roof of the sunporch with icy undertones.

On the floor at Gabby's feet, Annie whined softly. Like Theo, the dog hated anything out of the ordinary, anything that required an adjustment on her part, even a change in the weather. "It's all right, Annie," Gabby said, turning around and blocking out the gloomy specter beyond her windows. "We'll build a fire and snuggle on the couch. How's that?" The dog gave a halfhearted wag and raised her massive self by stages off the Navajo rug. Gabby patted her massive head then went through the shadowed halls to the living room, the dog padding silently behind her.

The living room was shaded in twilight; the furniture, darker shades of shadows when Gabby pushed the heavy carved doors open on the immaculate room. She flipped a porcelain switch on the wall and turned on the Tiffany floor lamps as well as the lights on the Christmas tree in the corner then crossed to the brick fireplace. It only took her a minute to strike one of the long fireplace matches she kept in a brass container on the mantle and get the cured wood burning. Satisfied that the fire would catch, Gabby looked around for her book. It was on the Queen Anne table where she had left it the night before.

The dog was already on the couch, waiting with an expectant look on her face as Gabby picked up the book. The house was silent and waiting around her; the fire began to cast friendly shadows across the oriental carpets, the sleet and rain a distant threat beyond the wide front porch filled with white wicker furniture, as Gabby joined the dog on the couch.

The lights on the Christmas tree twinkled bravely through the increasing gloom and caught the gold lettering on a small jewelry box still sitting on the heirloom tree skirt. Like the book Gabby held, the contents of the box were another present from Sam. "They're to replace those old pearl ones you've worn for a hundred years," Sam had told her on Christmas morning, as she unwrapped the box from Tiffany's and found the delicate pearl-and-diamond earrings inside. *Not a hundred years, Sam,* Gabby had thought, *only seventeen. They were a gift, not replaceable, not even with yours.* Gabby had put the new ones on only until Sam left, then switched back to the ones she wore now.

A sharp gust of wind rattled the shutters. The last leaves of winter flew past the side windows, looking dark and menacing through the leaded stained glass. The glider on the porch was rocked by some unseen hand and thudded against the clapboard siding. The noise startled Gabby, and she realized she was sitting on the couch beside the dog, staring at the tree and its presents, while she let herself slip into the solemn introspection this day always brought her. She was also putting off opening the book again. She had started it the night before when TV programming bored her, and she hadn't the energy to continue work in her studio. Only one chapter into the story and she had to put it aside because the pain of the story was all too familiar to her. *How appropriate,* Gabby thought. *Saving it to read today, this anniversary day.*

The book was the latest best seller—praised by the critics, read by millions, already sold to Hollywood. Gabby had purposely ignored it until Samantha had given it to her on Christmas Day. Somehow, that seemed an omen to Gabby, a sign that she needed to overcome her trepidation and read this story of star-crossed lovers and their compelling affair. *A fitting way to start off my own secret celebration of grief,* Gabby thought.

With a last look at the storm gathering strength outside, a last reassuring pat for the dog, and a strange mixture of reluctance and anticipation, she finally opened the book to the place she had closed it the night before. All through the remainder of the dark afternoon, Gabby read while the fire blazed, and the dog slept beside her.

It was after eight when Theo finally got home. He was delayed leaving Chicago by the storm then delayed again when his plane tried to land again in Knoxville. The Alberta Clipper was following the jet stream across the country and wreaking its usual December havoc on air travel.

Gabby greeted Theo then fixed soup and sandwiches while he unpacked. She wanted to get dinner over with as quickly as possible. Now that she had committed herself to her reading, the book seemed to beckon her, seduce her, and dare her to finish it. Theo didn't seem to notice. As always, he was just glad to be home.

Once they had eaten and exchanged brief reports on their almost-a-week apart, Theo put the dishes in the dishwasher while Gabby set the coffee up for morning. It was a routine born over years of practice. That finished, they settled companionably in the living room. Theo switched the TV on, the dog settled herself back on the couch, and Gabby picked up her book again. Two hours later, two endless and painful hours later, she turned the final page.

Over the muted voices on the TV, Gabby could hear the ticking of the grandfather clock in the hall. The dog snuffled and twitched in her sleep. Theo chuckled at something in the book he was reading. To outward appearances, it was just another night—a night like hundreds of others shared by Gabby and Theo.

Only Gabby knew differently. As she stared past the room and its familiar shapes and shadows at the fire, the flickering flames became kaleidoscopic prisms refracted by her tears and filmed in shocking Technicolor. The last thing Gabby wanted to do was sit there in her perfect living room and cry silently. Her grief, accelerated by the book, had started for real. Gabby wanted to scream at the gods, rant at the heavens, fall on the floor, and sob until she was exhausted and had no tears left. She wanted to cry until her eyes were as empty as her soul.

She couldn't allow herself that indulgence. The reason for her yearly descent into pain and memories was the one and only secret she had from Theo. Gabby glanced across the room at her husband of thirty-one years and wondered if keeping it had been worth the pain that it caused her.

Theo sat in his easy chair, his feet up on the matching ottoman, reading the latest Tom Clancy and watching something on the Discovery Channel. He was totally oblivious to Gabby. *Yes,* Gabby decided. *Of course it was worth it. It had to be. Otherwise, I've wasted seventeen years of my life.* Gabby knew she could explain the quiet tears pooled on her lower lids and distorting her vision by telling Theo it was a sad book. He was used to that. Gabby cried at christenings and weddings, when she saw sad movies or read sad books, and sometimes, for no apparent reason at all.

Like most men, Theo learned to accept that. And also like most men, he never really understood it. The racking, terrifying anguish Gabby felt was something Theo could never accept. And the reason was she felt it would destroy him and their carefully built life together. That was why, for the past seventeen years, Gabby lived with her secret tucked safely away in a misty corner of her heart. Evidently, Theo finally felt Gabby's gaze on him because he looked up. A slight frown creased his familiar forehead. "You all right?" "Sad book," Gabby said, looking away from him and back at the fire. Theo shook his head in resignation and went back to his reading.

Yes, she thought. *Unbearably sad book, Theo,* Gabby thought, *and so close to true.* Parallel lives—she remembered the long-ago phrase. Seventeen years earlier, Gabby and a man named Dr. Graham Wright had made the same painful decision the lovers in the book made. Graham had commitments and responsibilities. Gabby had commitments, responsibilities, and four young children. They were two people caught up in something they never expected to experience. And in the end, they were unable to rip apart innocent lives to be together.

Today was the anniversary of the last time Gabby's eyes met Graham's, the last time she heard his voice, the last time she felt his touch. It was the anniversary she endured each year.

Annie got up, stretched, and went to the door. Gabby saw it as a much-needed escape. "I'll take her," Gabby said, getting up and fighting back the sobs caught deep in her throat. *If I can only hold off until I'm outside...*

"You sure?" Theo asked.

"Positive. The fresh air will feel good tonight."

"Thanks."

Theo was always telling Gabby how much he appreciated her taking up the slack when business demanded his presence out of town, as well as the concessions she made whenever he first got home tired and, too often, grumpy. In keeping with long-ago promises to herself, Gabby willingly did that and more to make life as easy as possible for Theo. She felt she owed him that. Theo had asked her once, years earlier, if she were trying to atone for something terrible she had done in another life by being so thoughtful in this one. He had meant it as a joke. Gabby never told him why the question had made her cry.

She slipped her feet into the hot-pink flats that matched the pink-and-navy plaid shirt she wore with her old jeans, then went to the closet in the foyer, got out her oversized denim jacket, and shrugged into it. At the carved and ornate front door, Annie watched her with expectant eyes. "I may be a while." Gabby leaned around the corner of the french doors between the foyer and the living room and told Theo, "I think I'll walk her longer than usual, get her to settle down for bedtime."

"Good idea," Theo said, his eyes never leaving his book.

Must be an exciting chase scene, Gabby reasoned, going to the front door and snapping the leash on Annie. *I should've read something like that this afternoon instead of what I read.*

Outside, the air was cold, colder than Tennessee usually got. The wind whipped around Gabby as soon as she stepped through the door. Earlier, the winter storm warnings were extended to cover the entire Tennessee, North Carolina, and Georgia region. The afternoon's chilly rain was already sleet, and Gabby knew it would turn to snow quickly now, as the temperatures dropped.

The mountain passes to the south at Monteagle, as well as the ones to the North and the gateway to the Cherokee National Forest, were already closed. The Smoky Mountains were now inaccessible, and the freeway into Asheville and the Blue Ridge Parkway had shut down hours ago.

Gabby paused long enough to turn her jacket collar up then crossed the porch and went down the walk, led by the prancing black-and-white dog. Down six steps, through the old, ivy-covered retaining wall, and they emerged on the city sidewalks. Both sides of the street were lined with huge, old Victorian homes surrounded by ancient trees. Gabby glanced up at the dark sky. It looked alive to her, twisting and writhing with the storm. Down the hill, the weak yellow glow of a streetlight gleamed ghostlike through the sleet. Fog rose from the ground under the light and mixed with the swirling mists descending from the winter sky. Fog always made a viselike grip tighten around Gabby's heart. Tonight was no exception. It brought back all the memories of Boise.

The last of the dead and crumpled leaves on the huge maples gave up their final hold on black and skeletal branches as Gabby started down the sidewalk behind the dog. The leaves fell, caught the windy updrafts, then whirled in a final crazy dance before they came to rest on the cold, wet ground. Gabby saw it all from a distance, distracted and removed, lost in old, old feelings and this year's fresh pain. Every day for seventeen years, she thought of Graham. Even now, standing in the blowing sleet with the dog waiting impatiently on the familiar sidewalks, Gabby could feel his hands on her body and his kiss on her lips—feel them just like she had every day of her life since they parted.

California
Thursday, December 22, 1976

Will someone wiser than I ever hope to be
please tell me, is this all there is?

The bright California sunshine lit Dr. Graham Wright's study as he put his notes in the old and battered leather briefcase he'd had since graduate school. His wife, Patti, leaned in the doorway and pouted as usual. Patti had yet to figure it out, even though they'd been married six years. Graham had to go, no matter how difficult she made it, as he now tried, once again, to explain. "Patti, it's what I do. I give lectures. I talk to people who want to hear what I have to say. And I do it when they want me to."

"I know," Patti said. "But it's almost Christmas."

"I'll be back. Good Lord." Graham's irritation threatened to surface. He struggled to control it before continuing in a more patient voice. "It's Thursday, Patti. I'll be home Saturday."

"That's Christmas Eve. And you have to leave again on Monday for that stupid seminar."

"Patti, please," Graham said softly. "Let's not do this every time I leave town. You know I have to fit the speaking engagements and the seminars in when I have a break from teaching my classes."

"I'll miss you."

"And I'll miss you," Graham answered, trying not to let it sound as perfunctory as he felt. The petulant tone Patti used was grating on his last nerve. Even so, he gave her a quick peck on the cheek when he passed her, anxious to get to the airport without rushing. "I'll call you when I get to Boise."

When Graham finally escaped the house, he breathed a sigh of relief. He stowed his bags in the trunk of the car, got in, started the motor, and then backed out of his Nasturtium-bordered driveway. Once out of his comfortable neighborhood, Graham traveled up the freeway entrance ramp and headed west. The freeways were crowded, as usual. Luckily, it was a familiar route, and he could slip his mind into autopilot and let his thoughts wander.

As far back as Graham could remember, life fascinated him, challenged him, and involved him. Its infinite possibilities left him speechless. Only recently had it begun to seem a little empty. Restlessness had taken control, and Graham longed to know more, see more, do more, and be more. He wanted to find out what was in the world beyond his borders and see what it had to offer. *Midlife crisis, asshole,* he thought. *Shape up. Tame that restless seeker of truth gnawing at your soul.* Forty-five minutes later, at the airport, Graham parked his car and hurried to the gate. The flight to Boise was on time, and he was early. He watched his fellow travelers and allowed himself to wonder briefly where all the dreams had gone. When he and Patti had married, Graham had had the same expectations he assumed most grooms had: companionship, comfort, and someone to share his life and raise the children they'd one day have. By the end of his first year with Patti, Graham realized her idea of marriage was being joined at the hip like Siamese twins. And instead of raising children, Graham was raising Patti. When they were first married, Graham tried to get Patti to go with him when he lectured. But Patti was an aspiring actress who spent her days waiting for the call from her agent that would change her life and make her a star.

It was a call Graham doubted would ever come. Patti wasn't hungry enough to make it happen. Like everything else, she wanted stardom handed to her on a silver plate. She didn't want to pay the dues necessary to get there on her own. Lately, Graham had made a depressing discovery. He had married too late in life, and he had married someone too young. It was a moot point at this stage. Graham was an honorable man, brought up that way in his native South Carolina by God-fearing and ordinary people. Had he gotten his high school sweetheart pregnant in the back of his '51 Chevy, he would have married her and made the best of it. That was his nature. The same sense of responsibility and honor made him stay with his marriage, despite its shortcomings and his recent longings for something more.

Dr. Graham Wright taught ethics, specifically, ethics in business, to graduate students at USC. And it wasn't by accident he was drawn to that field. It suited him perfectly. Besides, he'd reasoned late one night, sitting up after Patti was asleep, nursing a Jack Daniel's on the rocks, when he looked at the marriages of his friends and fellow professors, they didn't seem all that different from his. Graham was still aware of life's infinite possibilities. Unfortunately, each year that passed seemed to remove more of them from his grasp.

"Eastern flight 115, nonstop to Boise, now boarding at gate 26." Graham stood, picked up his briefcase and his leather carry-on, then joined the other passengers for boarding. A friend of his, an older man whose advice Graham respected, once told him, "Love dies and is replaced with habit. It's all we can expect." Graham was beginning to believe that was true. He had married Patti when he was thirty-three because he had suddenly realized he wasn't getting any younger and it was time to settle down. To him, that marriage was a till-death-do-us-part, 100 percent commitment. And Dr. Graham Wright didn't take his commitments lightly.

Boise
Thursday, December 22, 1976

Most decisions are not made from wisdom but from expedience.

Gabriella (Gabby to everyone she met) Franks, thirty-four and running late, made a dash for the phone on her desk in the immaculate kitchen. She was almost out the door when it started ringing and had to drop her coat and briefcase on a chair and hurry back to the kitchen.

Outside the big bay windows with their Boston ferns hanging in brass planters, the day was gray and cold. The wind whipped the clouds around the far peaks of the Boise front, a preface to what was coming. Winter was late in Boise that year. According to the most recent weather reports, it would arrive that evening, with at least six inches of snow predicted before morning. "Hello?" Gabby was aware that she sounded a little irritated at the interruption.

"Did I almost miss you?"

Gabby smiled and dropped down in the chair beside the rolltop desk. "Theo, you have lousy timing. I have an ad meeting at nine, and I'm late already." Theo chuckled. Gabby knew why. She was always running late. It was her nature to cram too much into each and every day. She did it because she was afraid she might miss something exciting. Even the demands of her successful career at Lord and Young's, one of the city's most elite of stores, or being both a wife to Theo and a mother to their children, didn't tire her out or use up her excess store of energy. She was the perfect example of the saying "If you want something done, give it to a busy person."

"Have you talked to your folks?" Theo asked her.

"Last night."

"How are the kids?"

"Fine. Enjoying Christmas vacation with Grandma and Grandpa. How's New York?"

"Cold, snowing. Dirty."

"What else is new, huh? How are your meetings going?"

"Predictable. Look, I won't keep you. I just wanted to catch you before you left for work. Make sure everything was all right."

"Of course it is." Gabby smiled again. *Not that I'd tell you if it were not. In fourteen years of marriage, I have learned a few things, my dearest Theo,* she thought. *You want to hear everything is fine and good and normal. You hate problems.*

"Good. Good. Well, I'll try to call again tonight."

"Don't forget, I'm taking the training class to that lecture at Boise State tonight."

"Ah. I had. What time will you be home?"

"Who knows? Later than I want to be, that's for sure. But dear old Jack arranged for us to have coffee and conversation with the lecturer, somebody by the name of Dr. Graham Wright, afterward."

"Sounds good. Well then, I guess I'll wait and call in the morning."

"That's probably going to be less frustrating for both of us," Gabby admitted. Theo believed in early to bed, so even with the time change from eastern to mountain time, asking him to call when she got home would force him to stay up past his bedtime. "Tomorrow morning, then."

"Tomorrow morning." Gabby hung up the phone, gathered up her things, and hurried out of the house.

Years earlier, when Gabby said "I do," she expected to share her whole life with Theo. She knew he had problems with intimacy, shied away from emotional scenes, and gave an initial impression of cool, calculated control, but thought they could work around that. She'd just have to take it easy and not rush or pressure him. But as their life together wore on and as Gabby held back her feelings to accommodate Theo's, she realized his walls were very permanent and much too thick to ever be broken down. She also realized Theo gave her as much as he could of himself. Quite simply, what he gave was all he had to give. If she sometimes felt sorry for herself, Gabby felt even sorrier for Theo. In the imaginary book she would have written, he missed far too much of what life had to offer. Over the years, their lives, while fulfilling and exciting, grew to be almost totally separate.

Still, Gabby decided, what she had wasn't all that bad. She wasn't content to sit home and wait for Theo to magically appear on weekends, fresh from some business trip or the other, and tell her about his week. Not even with four kids, now ages eight to thirteen. She got grumpy and bitchy staying home alone while he traveled. There was a world out there, and she needed to be part of it.

Luckily, because of who and what he was, Theo didn't mind. It took the pressure to be intimate with his solitary life off his shoulders. He loved her. Gabby knew that. He loved the children. They knew that. His ultrastrict German and religious upbringing prevented him from showing much warmth and emotion. Gabby finally decided Theo was good at the motions of living but short on the know-how to feel what it was really like. As soon as she accepted that, Gabby tried to respect his feelings and make no demands on him that he was uncomfortable with. She knew Theo had married her because she was different from the other girls he dated. From the beginning of their sophomore year at college, Gabby enthralled Theo by doing all the crazy things he only dreamed about. And in the end, Gabby decided, she didn't really mind that either. Lord knew she had enough zest for life to satisfy both of them.

But best of all, in Gabby's mind, Theo never tried to tame her enthusiasm and never tried to make her stay home. Because of that, Gabby tried very hard to live within the parameters Theo found safe and acceptable. Truth be told, Gabby had married Theo because he was the fourth person to ask her in four years and the only one she didn't think would clip her wings until she couldn't fly anymore. Besides, college had been almost over. It had been time to get married. Gabby never regretted her decision.

Tennessee
December 30, 1993

*I wonder if you miss something you've never had.
Or are you content to live in the zombie world
of nothingness with everyone else?*

Gabby barely felt the sleet on her face and didn't notice her shoes were soaked through. She wasn't on this Tennessee Street in December 1993. She was back in time in Boise, December 1976. Finally she was far enough away from the house to sob convulsively and knew the dog was the only one who could hear her. Even the dog would have trouble because of the gusting wind.

"Where are you, Graham?" Gabby whispered through her tears. "How are you? Have you had a good life?"

Do you still feel my touch like I feel yours, Graham? Like I will feel it until the end of my life? Do you still remember the scent of my body as I do yours? They were the same questions Gabby asked every year on this day.

Annie paused beside an ice-rimed shrub and squatted. Annie was named Annie because she was an anniversary present from Theo. Annie was the nickname for Anniversary Dog. Gabby had laughed when Theo brought the gangly puppy home; she had told him most women got diamonds for their anniversary. Theo had kissed her cheek and reminded her she didn't wear jewelry, except for that old pair of pearl earrings. Besides, since she wasn't working anymore, the dog would be company and diamonds wouldn't. Theo was nothing if not logical. Finished with her business, Annie shook the condensation off her shiny coat and looked at Gabby as if to say, "Is this enough of this idiocy? Can we go back now?"

"Not yet, Annie. I can't do it yet," Gabby tried to explain. "I can't act normal just yet. I'm sorry."

It was a good life Gabby and Theo lived—comfortable and safe, thoughtful and caring. It was the life Gabby always knew they'd live if she didn't blow it. Their four children were grown and gone, well employed and well into their lives. She and Theo had three grandchildren and another on the way.

During the long years of child rearing and the pursuit of her career, there were little joys and big joys in Gabby's life. There were little disappointments and big disappointments. At the advent of each of these, still in the midst of the celebration or the despair, the first thing Gabby wanted to do was call Graham. Her heart ached with the need to share the joys with him and have him hold her in his strong arms to ease the disappointments. Gabby took a deep breath. She didn't smell the wet sleet or the blowing wind. She smelled the musky, warm, masculine scent of Graham, even after all these years. It filled her nostrils and made her dizzy with needing him. Like it always had.

Boise
Thursday, December 22, 1976

Tennessee Home

He filled my senses with his presence then stole them
all away from me, never returning a single one.

Τhe only problem with not having anyone to really share your *life*, Gabby decided, as she hustled the last of the training class from Lord and Young's into the lecture hall at the local college, *is it sometimes feels so lonely and seems so damned futile. Stop it,* Gabby berated herself, going down the long aisle behind the class she was responsible for. *It's been a long day. You're tired, the weather's lousy, and you're feeling sorry for yourself because you have nothing but an empty house to look forward to tonight when you go home.*

As promised that morning, winter finally got to Boise. The six inches of predicted snow started around two, and already there were seven inches of slushy white stuff on the streets, and it was still falling. *So much for accuracy in weather predictions,* Gabby grumped. She took the aisle seat, crossed her long legs, then dug around in the Gucci briefcase she'd dumped by her feet until she came up with a legal pad to make notes on. Lord knew if she left it up to her class, there would be no questions for this Dr. Wright after his lecture on ethics in business, and they'd all look like idiots. The management trainees were already peeved at having to work during their Christmas vacation instead of going home for the holidays—no telling how sullen they would be after giving up tonight to hear a lecture.

Gabby had no sympathy for them. They knew what the on-the-job training consisted of when they signed up. She made sure of that. Still, she didn't want them to look like total asses at the coffee hour later. It reflected badly on the store and on their esteemed leader, namely, Gabby. It was the second year she'd been in charge of turning the class of college seniors who thought they wanted to go into retailing into management material. Twice a week, they had classes at Lord and Young's; the rest of the time, they attended Boise State or engaged in hands-on merchandising back at the store.

By the end of the school year, the class would know everything there was to know about the day-to-day management of a large department store—from receiving of merchandise to ringing out registers, from inventory control to profit-and-loss statements, from security to open-to-buy. And Gabby would be the one they learned it from.

The course had been her idea and duplicated the one she'd taken when she worked at Dayton-Hudson's in Minneapolis years earlier. When she brought it up to her boss, Jack Young, he'd thought it was an excellent idea and put Gabby in charge. He also promoted her to vice president in charge of merchandising.

Gabby always thought of her title as kind of a catchall phrase, especially knowing Jack as well as she did. Still, the money and the prestige were nice. And it looked great on her business cards in their eel-skin carrying case.

She gave the room around her a perfunctory glance. It was typical of auditoriums and lecture halls all over the world—plain, antiseptic, and void of style and charm. In front of the rows of pull-down seats, a podium stood on a small stage, a reading lamp affixed to its side. Fluorescent lights blazed overhead, casting a harsh light on the row of students Gabby brought with her. Luckily, once the lecture and coffee hour were over, her responsibilities ended. Once dismissed, all her trainees had to do was walk across the campus to their dorms.

Flipping open her appointment book, Gabby jotted down some notes for the next day while they waited for the lecture's eight o'clock starting time. She sensed movement on the stage then heard the voices around her become subdued until they were silent. Vaguely, she heard Dr. Wright introduced and hurried so she could direct her attention to the class.

There was more shuffling as Dr. Graham Wright took his place and gave a murmured "Thank you." Gabby smiled as soon as she heard his voice. It was low, well modulated, well educated, and seemed to caress the hall intimately. It was also tinged with the slightest Southern drawl. Gabby loved Southern accents, especially in men. They were so soft and gentle. She quit writing and looked up, more interested now. At least she could enjoy listening to this man, no matter how good or bad a speaker he turned out to be.

To Gabby's surprise, Dr. Graham Wright was looking straight at her. His stare was both surprised and intense, and the force of it made Gabby's heart pound and do some kind of crazy flip-flop thing against the thin wall of her chest. The air around her pressed inward until it constricted her breathing. Gabby knew why immediately. She hadn't been looked at like that since she was nineteen in college and driving her bright red MG with the top down, free and full of spirit.

Gabby's early lifetime of hopes and dreams had long been repressed in her marriage to Theo. Now they were screaming for release as they tumbled around her for the first time in years, restless inmates let out of a zoo. It was such a strange and forgotten sensation that Gabby was left feeling breathless and confused. Her only comfort was that the man looking at her so intently from the podium seemed as confused as she was. Gabby was sure this Dr. Wright had no more hints as to what was causing this sudden connection weaving and dancing between them than she had.

There was no way Gabby could look away, even if she wanted to. And she was by no means sure she wanted to. She felt her reasoning and her sanity float away, chasing after the fleeing inhabitants of the zoo. As Gabby sat there, mesmerized, ancient winds blew around her and warmed her body. The smoke from man's first fire eddied around the hall in gray-blue waves, collected in the corners, then rolled forward and smothered her. Her nostrils were filled with its sweet aroma.

Gabby tried to blame these strange feelings on the fact that she'd always had a vivid imagination as well as a flair for the dramatic. And this man had certainly tapped into it. Her imagination was running rampant with possibilities. Gabby felt like an embryo about to be born. Between the staccato thumps her heart was making and her racing pulse, Gabby managed to check in with her brain long enough to realize she wasn't going to be able to turn her back on what was happening here. It was too intense. And it had been too long since she'd felt this way. Strange, she hadn't even realized that until tonight, looking into this stranger's eyes.

This stranger at the podium was no stranger at all but as familiar to Gabby as her own reflection; she felt like she'd stumbled and discovered that lost part of herself.

A forgotten line from a long-ago poem flitted across Gabby's brain, its words printed in flashing neon lights. "We sought each other long before we met." It described the way Gabby's soul felt. As quickly as the lights had come, they dissolved and were replaced by what she always thought of as the devil and the angel sides of her conscience. The little cartoon figures were carrying on a fearsome debate inside her head, arms flailing, heads bobbing, tiny feet stomping. They needn't have bothered. Gabby already knew who was going to win this one, and it wasn't her angel.

She had left the house that morning after talking on the phone to Theo, then had gone to work at the store, made it through her day there. Then she had gathered up the motley assortment of students in her training class and driven to Boise State, content and complacent in the belief that her life wasn't lacking anything at all. Watching Graham on the stage, Gabby realized it was lacking something. It was lacking him. She had a sudden intake of breath with the realization. Suddenly, Theo was only a vague memory in her distant past. Her mind rebelled ever so briefly at that thought while her angel conscience made a last, desperate stand.

Taking a deep, much-needed breath, Gabby accepted the fact that the man on the podium, this Dr. Graham Wright, was about to become the biggest influence on her life of anyone she'd ever know. It was written on ancient scrolls, carved in volcanic stone, and destined from the beginning of time. Gabby sat in her chair at the end of the row in the middle of the lecture hall and accepted it unconditionally. She didn't even pretend to make notes after that. Instead, she watched Graham.

God, he's gorgeous, she thought. *He is intelligent, sexy, and at least six foot four, with shoulders broad enough to balance the world—my world, at least.* Gabby imagined her angel conscience pouting behind the bars of a cage in the recently abandoned zoo while her devil conscience cavorted with the freed inmates. *Wonder what his arms will feel like when they close around me, how the weight of his body will feel against mine.*

Shocked at where her thoughts ended up and how quickly they got there, Gabby tried valiantly to pull herself back from the edge of indecency. Looking at Graham made that task almost impossible. His golden-brown hair was curly, a little long at the collar, and tumbled carelessly around a face that looked strong but which Gabby knew could, would, be gentle. Even across the distance between them, the deep hazel-green eyes fixed on hers captivated Gabby.

Graham made a brief gesture to underline something he said, and Gabby saw the gold band on his left hand. It didn't matter. She wore one of those too. And it had nothing to do with what has happening between them. There was an unspoken question in the eyes Graham turned back on Gabby. Before she realized what she was doing, she nodded. Just once, just briefly. It was enough. Graham nodded back the same way. He looked down at his notes then and gave Gabby the chance to reclaim the space around her. He would never let her reclaim her soul. Already, Gabby knew she would never want to.

At the end of the lecture, a lecture Gabby barely heard, Graham came down the two steps and into the audience. He shook the offered hands and accepted the words of thanks and praise while looking over the heads of the people, always keeping Gabby in sight. Gabby simply stood there and waited. Slender strands, both as fragile and as strong as a spider's web, reeled her in and paralyzed her.

Gabby was a lot of things, but a fatalist wasn't one of them. She believed in free choice and free will. *So why in hell am I standing here, waiting for a stranger, feeling a connection to him that overshadows everything else in my life? Ready to risk everything I have just to be with him? Because you're losing your mind*, she answered herself. *You've finally slipped over the edge and become a complete, certifiable lunatic.*

"Mrs. Franks? Shall we meet you there?"

"What?" Gabby said. Her thoughts dissolved around her as she dropped back into her surroundings. One of the members of the training class was talking to her. "Shall we meet you there?" the student repeated patiently. To Gabby, he sounded like he was talking to a particularly difficult and half-deaf maiden aunt.

"There? Oh, you mean the cafeteria. Yes, it's straight across the campus. Big brick building with a couple of ugly statues in front of it," Gabby said distractedly. "Take everyone with you. I'll wait for Dr. Wright."

Gabby wondered why the student gave her such a strange look until she realized she'd just given him directions to the cafeteria on his own college campus. *Wonderful,* she thought. *The vice president of Lord and Young's is getting senile at the tender age of thirty-four. Old boss-man Jack will love that.* At last, Graham worked his way through the press of people and went straight toward Gabby. When he was no more than three feet away, he stopped.

Gabby felt like a drowning victim as Graham's eyes swept from her face to her feet and back again. The devil conscience perched on her shoulder now and laughed raucously. Trivial details assaulted her brain, like the fact that she wore her new suede suit that morning. It consisted of an ankle-length suede skirt with a matching oversized bomber jacket. Gabby wore it over an ivory cashmere turtleneck. The soft burnished-bronze skirt and jacket set off her streaky light-gold hair in its neat twist, just like she knew it would when she bought the outfit. Her hair was squeaky clean and perfumed. Her legs were shaved. Her long nails were perfectly manicured. *Stop this,* she chided herself. *You are not some piece of meat on a rack, hoping to be bought by this man.*

"Dr. Wright?" Gabby shook off her thoughts, as well as the little devil conscience perched on her shoulder, and managed to extend her hand. "I'm Gabriella Franks."

"I hoped you were," Graham said simply. He took the offered hand and held it much longer than convention allowed.

"Shall we go? I have my car outside. Or we can walk." Gabby felt suddenly flustered. It was an unusual state for her. The last time she'd felt that way, she was twelve and had forgotten the notes to Rachmaninoff's Third Concerto at her piano recital. "Unless, of course, you have a car? Then I can point you in the right direction."

"I took a cab," Graham said. "I'm not used to driving in the snow." He took her arm lightly, just above the elbow, and steered her toward the door. Gabby was intensely aware of his presence, his closeness. It made it hard to breathe.

On the broad steps, they stopped and Graham looked around. The snow still fell in a soft, sensuous curtain of white. Across the campus, the cafeteria glowed a welcome through the darkness. Only a few scattered lights were on in the dorms surrounding the quad. Most of the students had abandoned the campus to spend holidays with family or to head off on ski trips. The mercury glow of the lamps lining the walkway was a pale, subdued yellow as it fought to be seen through the falling snow. Other than the distant cafeteria that was their destination, the only other building showing any signs of life was the library. There was no one on the walkway, no one around any of the buildings. Gabby was reminded of a moonscape, otherworldly and strange. Like she felt. Like this Dr. Wright made her feel.

"Do you like walking in the snow?" Graham asked.

"As a matter of fact, I do."

"Good. So do I, although I don't get much of a chance at it." Without another word, his hand on Gabby's elbow propelled her down the steps and along the drifted walkways toward the distant lights. The forgotten packed snow crunched and squeaked under their feet.

"You're married," Graham said.

It was a statement, not a question, and far too personal an observation for him to be making. Gabby expected it—was, in fact, waiting for it.

"So are you," she said. "Does it matter?"

"No." There was no hesitation in Gabby's answer, no surprise shown at his question. Quite simply, it didn't matter. Not much did right now. Gabby glanced up at Graham, at his profile dusted by the falling snow and enhanced with a halo by the lights on the walkway. In that split second, she felt the world go through the pain of creation and spew him out, just for her. It was why she was born, why she existed, why she was here on this snowy night in Boise, Idaho.

She was awfully glad both sides of her conscience had retreated inside her brain, where they belonged, and were leaving her alone. She did think, however, it would be nice if she could remember the names of her children.

"This class," Graham said. "Will they keep us long?"

"Much too long."

"Any time at all is too long."

Tennessee
December 30, 1993

There is no solace for a heart once broken, never mended.
There are, forevermore, the shadows of the broken parts.

Annie whined, and Gabby ignored her. If only she had someone to talk to when the feelings overtook her and threatened to bury her in sadness. She'd reasoned it over by herself so many times over the years, having conversations with herself again and again.

"Tell me, Gabby, do you regret the decision to stay in your world, your marriage, your life?"

"Well, Gabs, no more, no less, than I regret making the decision to leave."

"Well, Gabby, would you explain that to me, please?"

"Sure, what's so very hard to understand and accept is that from the first moment Graham and I fell so heartbreakingly in love, we were in a no-win situation. Damned if we did, damned if we didn't. Either way meant pain. We chose to bear the pain ourselves, rather than ask innocent people to do it. How do you regret a decision like that?"

The sleet lashed at Gabby as, lost in her memories, she continued to drag the unwilling dog down the sidewalk. It was getting colder with every minute they were out, every faltering step they took. The wind blew the sleet sideways across Gabby's vision, sent it slapping into her face, stinging painfully where it mixed with her tears.

There were no cars on the roads now, very few lights shining in the houses they passed. Now, for the first time in the past seventeen years, Gabby thought about walking until she dropped. Let them find her cold, stiff, decidedly dead body when the snow melted. She rejected the idea as quickly as it came. Doing that would mean the last seventeen years—all her struggles, all her pain—had been for nothing. Plus it would devastate the family she'd sacrificed herself to keep intact. It would invalidate the secret she'd worked so hard and so long to keep. Besides, tonight the dog would freeze. Gabby knew she'd never be able to die with that on her conscience.

At the next side street, Annie balked. She planted herself firmly on the icy curb and refused to go another step away from the safety, comfort, and warmth of home. Since the dog outweighed Gabby by at least fifty pounds, she really had no choice. Reluctantly, she turned around and headed back in the direction they'd come.

The streetlights reflected off Gabby's pale-gold hair as they retraced their steps. It was silver-streaked now, and lines were beginning to show in her sculptured face. But the cheekbones were still as high as ever, and the eyes were the same piercing blue they'd always been.

Graham once told her those eyes reflected every summer sky he'd ever seen. Gabby could hear him say it, hear his voice curl around her senses, as he added, "A man could really drown in them," as she heard the softness in his drawl.

She heard it in the wind, heard it in the rain, and heard it in the drone of insects on a summer's night. She heard it in silence, heard it in the roar of the sea. And always, always, she heard it in her dreams. Gabby loved the way Graham talked, loved the way his voice wrapped around the words, making them sound so special, like he made her feel. She could hear that voice tomorrow, across a room, across a canyon, across the world, and know before she turned to look, that it was Graham speaking.

Boise
Thursday, December 22, 1976

This heart you might not trouble, but you did.
This life you might not shatter, but you did.
This love you might not conquer, but you did. You did.

"Ethics in business," Graham told one of the trainees around the large round table in the student cafeteria. "It's no different from ethics in anything else. It defines who we are." "Sets our limits," Gabby added. Graham nodded and stirred his coffee. One of the trainees had been thoughtful enough to have two extra cups of the steaming liquid, drawn from the large silver urns beside the cashier's desk, waiting for Gabby and Graham when they got there. *Just made it too,* Gabby thought as she watched the weary cashier count out her register, prepare the bank deposit, and close down her station for the night. *Otherwise, we'd be stuck with the mud that passes for coffee in the vending machines.*

"Yes, ethics," Graham said, "sets our limits and tells the world who we really are."

Despite her earlier worries, the discussion was moving along at a fast clip. To Gab's utter amazement, the group of trainees had actually listened to the lecture Graham given. *It's a good thing,* she thought. *I certainly didn't.* As Graham spoke, she watched him, her eyes tracing every inch of his features. Her coffee grew cold in the cup she held in her hand, and she didn't even notice. She was more concerned with catching the nuances of Graham's expressions, the passion in his face when he spoke.

The other students who'd chosen, for reasons of their own, to stay at the college during their vacation, straggled in and out of the cafeteria, getting candy bars, canned soups, and soft drinks from the bank of colorful vending machines along the wall. Their chatter and laughter, along with the rattle of change and the thumps of the vending machines, competed with Graham's voice, at times almost drowning him out. Gabby didn't notice that either.

"Dr. Wright, are there ever exceptions? Times when something might be all right, something you wouldn't usually do?" It was a question from one of Gabby's brighter trainees.

"Extenuating circumstances, you're asking?" Graham paused while tamping down the tobacco in his pipe, then held a match to it and inhaled deeply. The scent of his tobacco was the most sensuous thing Gabby ever remembered smelling. *Stop it,* she fussed at herself. *You are getting out of hand here. I think this is what you called a case of raging hormones back in college.*

"I suppose that's what I mean," the trainee shrugged.

Graham thought about that while he got his pipe going to his satisfaction. "Do you mean in business or in life?" he finally asked quietly.

"Is there a difference?"

"There wouldn't be if this were a perfect world. We set a standard for ourselves. A standard we plan to live our life by. Run our business by. A line we think we'll never cross. Certainly don't intend to cross. Will we someday cross it?" Graham looked away from the trainee and directly into Gabby's eyes again. "Depends on how strong the motivation is to step across into uncharted areas. To go where we've never been before and never thought we'd go. To go to a place we never knew or even suspected existed. It depends on the time, the place, and the people involved."

"What if it hurts innocent people?" Gabby asked softly, partly for her students' benefit but mostly for herself.

"You must try very hard not to let that happen," Graham answered. "You do your best to protect them."

"At what cost?" a student asked.

"I can't answer that," Graham said. "When that day—that time—comes, then we will know, but not now, not yet."

Gabby drew in a deep breath and felt the impact of his warm eyes and soft voice consume her. Every nerve in her slender body seemed to be sticking through her skin, longing toward him and yearning for his touch. *Oh, the heck with this stupid masquerade,* she decided. *I have got to get out of here.*

"Thank you, Dr. Wright," she said, hoping her voice didn't give away what she was feeling. "In light of the weather and the fact that tomorrow is a working day at the store, I think we all need to bring this to a close."

"I agree." Graham smiled at her.

That smile lit up the dormant soul of my personal Sleeping Beauty, she thought. *Awakened now after her long sleep.*

"If I could trouble you for a ride?" Graham continued.

"Of course."

Around them, the latest of scholars and bravest of students had finally abandoned the Boise State cafeteria for the shelter of their dorm rooms. Gabby's little group represented the only sign of humanity left.

She stood up, effectively ending the session and giving her charges permission to leave. She watched as the twelve trainees gathered up their things, loaded backpacks or briefcases, said their good-byes, and started for the door. Once the students were gone, Gabby gathered up the dirty cups and placed them on a tray.

"Want help?" Graham asked.

"Not with this." She started toward the little window outside the kitchen, where dirty dishes were left. Graham smiled at her again, picked up her jacket and her briefcase, and then followed her across the cafeteria. After she put the cups down, he held her jacket for her then handed her the briefcase and took her arm again. Even at this time of night, the cafeteria was brightly lit. Every inch of it screamed *institution*. Now that the trainees were gone, it was deserted, save for one elderly man lethargically pushing a mop bucket and dragging a wet mop across the tiled floors. If erasing the evidence of dirty footprints and melting snow was his goal, he was doing a terrible job of it.

The snow was still falling, blowing across the open campus and creating uneasy drifts along the cleared walks, when Graham and Gabby stepped back out into the night. It floated down through the soft glow of the lights, looking mysterious and magical as they walked back toward the lecture hall and the parking lot where Gabby left her car.

"Are you worried about the cost we will have to pay?" Graham asked. His touch on Gabby's arm was burning her through the suede jacket.

"Yes, aren't you?"

"Not enough for us to stop where this is headed, even if I thought I could."

"Where is it headed?" Gabby asked.

"Anywhere it wants to go, I think."

"You make it sound like we have no choice."

Graham took a deep breath and looked down at Gabby seriously.

"I'm not sure we have one, are you?"

"No. No, I'm not. And if there is a choice we have, I'm trying hard not to find it."

"Good. So am I."

They got to Gab's car, and she opened the passenger door for Graham then hurried around to the driver's side. He leaned across the seat and opened her door for her.

When she got in, she could smell his pipe in the closed car, mixed with something else, something rich and masculine. It filled her senses, made her head swim, made her shiver in anticipation. It was all she could do to keep the little devil contained in her head. *Children*, she reminded herself. *Children's names—ah, yes. First, there's Sarah.*

"Where are you staying?" is what she said aloud.

"Hanover House," Graham answered.

She nodded, and for a while, they drove in silence. Gabby

could feel Graham watching her in the glow of the dash lights. Her skirt was slit up the front almost to the tops of her thighs. When she drove, it moved apart, giving him enticing glimpses of her long legs. She didn't try to close it. Her movements were efficient and practiced; her driving through the threatening weather was sure, precise, and even.

"Where did you learn to drive in snow?" Graham finally asked. "Here in Boise?"

"Minnesota." Gabby glanced at him and felt her heart in her throat again. *Now leave me alone,* she thought, I'm trying to remember my children's names. *Let's see—hum now—after Sarah, there was Susan. Yes, that's right, now keep your mind on your business, and keep driving.*

"Is that your home?"

"Now it is. My parents are there. I went to college there. Met my husband there."

"Got married there," Graham said softly.

"Yes."

"Children?"

"Four."

"Four?"

"Four." She laughed at the incredulous tone in his voice.

"All born there?"

"Yes." Gabby glanced over at Graham again. *Samantha—yes, that was it—Sam was the next child. Now if you stop the car and attack him here, you'll both freeze to death. Think of the headlines in the morning.*

"You?"

"Children?" Graham shook his head. "No. My wife is an actress."

Gabby laughed again. "Is that supposed to explain it?"

"To her it does."

"OK," Gabby said slowly. "Whatever, do I know her?"

Graham mentioned Patti's name, a couple of guest shots she'd done, a couple of sitcoms, and a small part in a best-forgotten movie. Gabby pumped her brakes and let the car glide to a stop at a red light then looked over at Graham in surprise. His words conjured up the picture of a petite, smiling brunette with a mass of shiny curls and a talent for comedy. "Patti Wright, of course. I do know of her. Well, I mean, I know who she is."

"Do you? I'm married to her, and I don't know who she is."

"I'm sorry." The light changed, and Gabby eased the car across the snow-compacted intersection.

"Me too," Graham said.

"This isn't about her, is it?"

"No," Graham said. "This is about you and me."

"Good," Gabby replied.

Jay was the last child. Her only boy, heir to Theo's good name—*Theo who? Oh yes, my husband.*

Even with the snow, it only took a scant fifteen minutes before the outskirts of Boise slid into view. The town was dark and deserted, the stores all closed. The Christmas decorations strewn across the intersections and draped down the light standards looked lost and forlorn as the wind whipped them back and forth at will. The gaily colored lights twinkled bravely through the thick curtain of snow as Gabby turned the car in the direction of the Hanover House. Once there, Gabby parked the car without even asking if she should and got out with Graham.

The snow, as was often the case in Boise, gave rise to a massive and all-concealing fog. It rose around Graham's and Gabby's bodies as they headed toward the entrance, a welcome cocoon of softness against the circling spirits and demanding need.

"I suppose I should ask if someone is home waiting for you," Graham said as they fought their way across the parking lot. Ahead of them, the lights in the lobby served as bright and cheery beacons. An elderly man in a red jacket with gold-braided roping decorating the shoulders hurried to open the doors as they approached. When he did, the ficus trees in the lobby beside the door shivered as the night air hit them.

"Evening," the doorman said.

"Good evening," Gabby replied, hurrying inside.

A bored desk clerk looked up from his newspaper as they blew into the lobby on a burst of icy wind. Graham nodded at the doorman, reached in his pocket, pulled out several crumpled bills, then handed them to the man. "Thank you, sir."

"There's no one waiting for me," Gabby said, picking the conversation up with Graham's last question. "Theo travels. The kids are at my parents' for Christmas vacation."

"Fate," Graham said softly. "Do I dare offer you a drink at the bar, or will someone recognize you?"

"Wouldn't matter if they did. My life is very much my own. I have a career. I have drinks with people. Have lunches and dinners with them, too. Even people of the opposite sex. So does Theo when he's out of town. So do I when I travel. That's business."

The desk clerk watched them cross the marbled floor of the lobby. The gilt chandeliers far above them tinkled softly in the leftover wind from the open door. As soon as the clerk saw them heading in the direction of the bar, he went back to his newspaper.

"This isn't," Graham said simply, "business."

"I know that. You know that. No one else has to."

The weather had pretty much cleared out the lounge Gabby and Graham entered. Its tiny tables were deserted, save for one intense couple against the back wall. From this distance, it was hard to tell if their intensity was a result of arguing or loving. Candles in hurricane lamps stood sentinel on the lonely tables and flickered bravely in the gloom. A solitary waitress leaned on the bar in conversation with a bartender who polished and repolished already-clean glasses.

Tips would not be good tonight, her demeanor said, *so why bother?* Once Gabby and Graham sat down, the waitress forced herself away from her flirtations with the bartender and meandered over to their table. Gabby ordered a margarita. Graham ordered Jack Daniel's on the rocks. A small combo played on the tiny stage in the corner, looking like they wanted nothing more than for the night to end so they could get out of there. Gabby and Graham listened in silence while they watched the waitress give the bartender their order, then put the glasses on a tray and start back toward them.

"Do you travel much?" Graham finally asked Gabby. The waitress got to the table and set down their drinks without a word. Then she turned and walked away. She too wanted to go home, preferably with the bartender, Gabby decided.

"New York market every couple of months," Gabby said.

"Not the California market?"

Gabby laughed softly. "Our customers aren't into California chic. They're much too elitist. They prefer the New York designers." She watched the candle play across Graham's handsome features and reflect in his dark-green eyes.

Graham smiled at her again. And Gabby melted again. *Much more of this,* she decided, *and I'm going to be nothing more than a puddle at his feet.*

"How'd you get into the rag trade?" he asked.

"Worked at Dayton-Hudson in Minneapolis when I was in high school and college. Daddy thought it would be good experience, being out in the business world. It got in my blood. Everything else seems so boring."

"You thrive on seventy-hour workweeks and Chinese fire drills?" *I can see that in you—you are full of everything about life.*

Graham's eyes in the dim light were full of age-old promise. Gabby didn't know if he was oblivious to the effect he was having on her or if he was just trying to keep some semblance of decorum around them with his conversation.

"Yes," Gabby said. "I guess I must."

"And still raise four children?"

"Well, I do have help. A dear friend and neighbor stays with the kids. A housekeeper comes in to clean up after all of us and leave meals that may or may not get eaten. I stayed home with them until they were all in school—they're eight, nine, eleven, and thirteen, now."

Boise Home

"The seventies woman, huh? Bring home the bacon and fry it up in the pan?" Graham quoted a familiar commercial line.

"If I had to, I have done it in the past," Gabby said seriously. "I don't have to anymore, there is Theo to help."

"Yes," Graham said, looking away. "Theo."

"Sorry," Gabby said.

Graham shrugged. "No matter. It's a fact of our lives, I'd say. We're both married."

It was Gabby's turn to ask. "Does that bother you?"

Graham was silent for a long time, pretending to listen to the barely adequate music emanating from the small stage.

"Everything about this bothers me," he finally said. "I'd much prefer to have met you when we were both single. When this could go someplace. When no one else was involved."

"So do we take what we've been offered?" Gabby's voice was soft and tentative. "Or do I go home?"

Graham looked back at Gabby; he said simply, "Your going back home is not even an option."

"I didn't think so. But I wanted to be sure."

"You can be very sure," Graham answered. "You're right where I want you to be."

Gabby's eyes twinkled. "Here in a bar? I could've sworn you had something more private in mind."

Graham laughed. "What are you doing now? Reading my mind?"

"It's my sideline," Gabby joked. "I put a sign outside the house when I'm not at the store. 'Palms read, fortunes told, minds read.' Like that."

Graham laughed again. "You haven't told me what you do at Lord and Young's."

"What I do, or what my title is?"

"There's a difference?

"Absolutely."

"Then both, I guess," Graham said.

"Well." Gabby took the smallest sip of her drink. It was cold, salty, and sharp, just the way she liked it. "My title says I'm vice president in charge of merchandising."

"But that's not what you do?"

"Oh, I do that, all right. And part of the buying, mainly for the two boutiques in the store. I also teach the class of trainees I had in tow tonight how to survive in the big, bad world of retailing. But most of the time, I think of myself as vice president in charge of Jack."

Graham laughed once more. Gabby got the impression it wasn't something he did often. "Jack is?"

"Jack Young," Gabby immediately answered. "Our esteemed leader. His parents started the store. Sometime back in the Middle Ages, I think. Thus the names. Young was Jack's father's name. Lord was his mother's maiden name. I guess they liked the sound of it. If Jack had named it, I'd say he was trying to capitalize on Lord and Taylor's. Or just being pretentious. But he didn't."

"But he does run it now?"

"He does. He went off to Harvard, got his degree in business management, then came back and took over. Since then, he's started opening other stores in Idaho, in Sun Valley, Pocatello, and Coeur d'Alene. He's also talking about expanding into other states. My job consists of following him around a lot and keeping him out of trouble. Also doing all the things he doesn't want to do. Oh yes, and some of the artwork for the ads as well."

"An artist too?"

"That's the other thing I want to be when I grow up."

Graham laughed. "I'm impressed," he said.

"I don't know why," Gabby said. "It's what I trained to do with my life."

Graham just shrugged. Gabby knew from his demeanor he wasn't used to a woman who went out and took what she wanted from life instead of waiting for someone to hand it to her. It made her wonder about his wife. She decided to change the subject. "And how about you, Graham Wright? Who are you? What do you do when you aren't flying around the country, lecturing to strangers?" *And accosting them from the podium,* she silently added. *Giving them the naughtiest of ideas.*

"I teach," Graham said. "Professor of ethics at USC. And I write."

"Anything I would've read?"

"Not unless you're into heavy and scholarly tomes about the decline and fall of ethics in the modern world."

"Now I'm impressed," Gabby said.

Graham didn't crack a smile when he said, "I don't know why. It's what I trained to do with my life."

"Touché," Gabby laughed.

They were quiet for a while, comfortably quiet. There weren't a lot of people Gabby felt easy about being quiet with. Not a lot of people she ever let her guard down with. Even fewer she felt she could be herself with instead of Gabriella Franks, wonder woman and retailer of purpose and brilliance. Feeling free to do so with Graham surprised her. She took another sip of her margarita while Graham watched her in the flickering light from the candle on the table.

"I've never done anything like this before," he finally said softly with tear-filled eyes.

"I know. Neither have I."

"I didn't want you to think—"

"I don't," Gabby assured him.

Graham reached across and took her hand. He twisted the wedding ring on her finger.

"It's what I want too, Graham," Gabby said. Her voice was barely a whisper. "I wouldn't be here if I didn't." Graham looked up from her hand. Gabby smiled at him, a smile of acquiescence and need. It was evidently what he needed to see because, as if in a dream or exaggerated slow motion, she saw his face moving toward her across the small table. She leaned in to meet him halfway. His first kiss was gentle and tender, and what little sanity Gabby had left was gone as soon as their lips met. Almost at once, the kiss became deep and filled with passion; Graham's lips were warm and searching, lost in the soft, willing depths of Gabby's mouth.

With the excitement and depth of the kiss, the feelings Gabby left in her youth came painfully back.

It was now what seemed like a century ago mixed with ancient and untested ones. By the time Graham pulled away, the room was spinning out of control around her. Just like she'd known it would.

"I think we should go upstairs," Graham said. Now his voice too was no more than a whisper in the night.

"So do I," Gabby said. "Before we embarrass ourselves in public."

As Graham led her out of the bar, their drinks sat almost untouched on the table, the ice melting and the napkins soggy. He, however, did remember Gabby's jacket and briefcase. She didn't.

Back in the sumptuous lobby, they passed the desk clerk again. This time he was watching TV and barely glanced up. A red runner led to the alcove where the elevators waited. Tropical plants stood on either side of the impressive doors, silent witnesses to the unfolding drama.

Graham pressed the up button, and almost immediately, a bronze door slid open. Gabby stepped into the elevator, and Graham followed. They rode up in silence, careful not to stand too close together. Gabby knew to do it would mean ending up a writhing, tangled mass on the carpeted floor of the elevator.

The elevator slipped to a silent stop on the third floor, and they made their way down the plush-carpeted hallway. Graham had his key out long before they reached his room. He opened the door and stood aside so Gabby could enter. She did so without the slightest hesitation.

The room was all cool grays and mauves. A crystal lamp was lit on either side of the bed. A Georgia O'Keefe reproduction in a heavy gilt frame hung over the ornate headboard. The maid who'd turned down the sheets had also left a chocolate on

Graham's pillow. The heavy drapes hanging over the french doors to the balcony were open, and Gabby could see the fog and snow swirling past.

She had been in a lot of hotel rooms, even stayed here at the Hanover House. But she'd never in her life been in one with any man but Theo. She was surprised at how natural and right it felt to be here with Graham. Walking into this room, Gabby realized, everything she'd innocently believed all her life, all she'd been taught, every rule she accepted and lived by, was left behind her. Even the disparate sides of her conscience had forged an uneasy truce, accepting her decision to be here.

She turned around and faced Graham. There was a question in his marvelous eyes. He stood still, giving her a chance to change her mind if that was what she wanted, Gabby knew.

"Hold me and make love to me, Graham," she said softly.

Graham's breath caught, and he closed the distance between them in milliseconds. He pulled Gabby into his arms and brushed her lips tenderly with his soft kiss, tasting her, learning her. One hand moved up the curve of her back. Gabby lost herself in the delicious sensation, just like she'd lost herself in him from the moment she first heard his voice.

Graham reached trembling hands up and took the pins out of her hair. It fell in a cascade of silk to several inches below her shoulders. She heard him catch his breath again. "I've wanted to do that all evening," he whispered against her hair. He stepped back, just slightly, still holding Gabby in his arms, while his eyes searched her face.

Gabby knew what he found there. Her clear-blue eyes were filled with a blind acceptance of where they were going and the need to go there. She used them to embrace his body and his soul as she sat on the edge of the bed and took her boots off.

Graham shrugged out of his tweed jacket with the suede patches on the sleeves. Then he watched while Gabby reached over and unbuttoned his shirt. She stood, pushed the shirt off his shoulders, and let it fall to the floor at his feet.

Gabby's hands moved slowly over Graham's muscled chest and arms, caressing him, exploring him. Graham ran a gentle hand down her cheek, as if he were memorizing the contours of her face. When he brushed a finger across her lips, Gabby took it and kissed it tenderly, delighting in its taste, scent, and texture. Then she took it in her hand and placed it on her body, moving to locations where she longed for it to be.

Her skirt snapped down the front, and discarding it was a simple matter of popping open a few snaps and letting it fall to the floor. Graham's hands shook almost uncontrollably as he undid each snap until the skirt fell and joined his shirt on the carpet.

Gabby wore a pair of soft pale-pink silk bikinis. Graham's breath was ragged in his throat as his hands closed over the perfect hipbones under her translucent skin.

Hands Gabby didn't recognize as hers reached for him. The rasp of his zipper was loud in the quiet room. Graham stepped out of his slacks, and Gabby brushed his skin with the lightest touch imaginable. In a trance, a dream, Gabby stepped back, reached for the bottom of her sweater, and pulled it over her head. Every fiber of her longed for and ached for the warmth of his touch.

Graham stood no more than six inches from her. Neither of them moved. Gabby knew they were crossing not those few inches but a chasm, a canyon she wasn't sure she'd ever get back across. Their sounds of breathing mingled in the quiet room. Graham's muscles caught in the shadows of the lamplight, and his need for her was a living, breathing presence around them.

Gabby was in the presence of something she'd never known before and would never find again. It was a third entity in the room with them. The world hung, reality suspended, and Gabby knew she was taking the first step on a journey she had never known and life had not prepared her for.

They made love in the glow of the lamps, and time was a ceaseless wonder. The planets swirled, and the earth split open. Age-old memories of the world's creation encompassed them and drove them ever further, ever closer and deeper. Gabby felt herself falling in love with Graham; it was not the passion the love talked about. It was the forever, that moment she felt the world as she knew it dissolve around her.

They floated above the earth in the swirling mists of a world beginning out of time. Darkness and light met in beautiful colors of falling meteors and unborn stars as their bodies strained together. From a great distance came the sound of rushing winds, tumbling waters, crackling fires. The animal-skinned figures of primitive man danced behind their closed eyes.

Gabby heard her breathing as she heard Graham's, distant and detached. It rose and fell in a crescendo of sweet ecstasy, trapped between the walls of canyons rising from the earth's molten crust.

Graham tenderly stroked Gabby's cheek as he traced every part of her flesh. After long, sweet moments, he spoke. "Will you stay?"

"Yes." Gabby wondered where else would she go, wondered, where else could she possibly find a love like this?

They made love again before they slept, then curled together, wrapped in each other's arms. They were alone in time and lost to the world. Outside, the falling snow continued to blanket the earth.

In the dark room, two souls blended and yearned for eternity. They didn't know it yet, but dying now would forever be so much easier than parting could ever be.

Tennessee
December 30, 1993

The world doesn't stop for anything or anyone.
It moves ceaselessly on, day after endless day.
Like a clock ticking in the darkness.

The sleet was snow as Gabby let the dog lead her back to the house. Big, fluffy flakes fell on her head, melting when they hit. They accumulated rapidly on the frozen ground. Annie nipped and snapped at them as they floated past.

"You dizzy dog, you can't catch a snowflake," Gabby said quietly. "And if you do, it'll melt." *Just like you can't hold on to a love that is rightfully yours,* she thought.

Over the years, Gabby had often wondered about the reason supposedly wise gods had for giving her something she couldn't keep. Why they saw fit to let her know what love was and, at the same time, give her too much decency and honesty to keep it.

At times, she consoled herself with knowing she had had it even for a painfully brief time. She loved and was loved in a way she knew most people never experienced. Tonight, that knowledge wasn't enough. Tonight, Gabby almost wished she'd never known what Graham brought to her life, almost wished she'd stayed blissfully ignorant and ordinary.

Almost, she thought, *just almost.* She never fully wished for that, no matter how bad the pain got. "I wouldn't have missed it for the world," Gabby whispered into the wind. "Wouldn't give back a single minute we had together, Graham."

Gabby was almost back to the house, where Theo waited. She could see its lights glowing softly like havens in the storm.

Wispy smoke filtered out of its brick chimney. It looked warm and welcoming and not at all like a prison for her soul.

"What I would give is the rest of my life. Just to hear his voice again. Just to lay my hand on his face," Gabby whispered. *Do you still drink Jack Daniel's, Graham? Do you still smoke your pipe with the tobacco you got from that little tobacco shop in Venice? I'll remember that smell always. As I remember every pleasure loving you brought me.*

Boise
Friday, December 23, 1976

*Lives change in an instant, in the blink of
time, never to be the same again.*

"Aren't you worried someone will say something about you coming to work in the same outfit you wore yesterday?" Graham asked.

They'd made love again as dawn broke over the snowy city. Gabby dressed reluctantly. Graham sat on the bed and watched. She got the impression he was memorizing her movements, storing them away to take out later.

"I work at a store, remember?" She jiggled her key ring at him. "I have keys to it. I'll pick out a new outfit, change into it, and have Jack put it on my charge when he comes in."

"Won't Jack wonder?"

"He can wonder all he likes. He'll never say anything to anybody." Gabby leaned over to kiss Graham.

"Why is that?" He captured Gabby in his arms and pulled her down across him.

She laughed. "Because I've covered his tracks too many times," she said.

"Buy you breakfast?"

"Don't eat it."

"Coffee?"

Gabby hesitated. "Let me go down first. Get a table. That way it will look like a chance meeting if anyone sees us."

Unwillingly, Graham let her go, and Gabby gathered up her

things to leave. The phone on his bedside table rang as she pulled his door closed behind her.

She knew without asking, without stopping to eavesdrop, that it would be his wife. Just like she knew her phone at home would ring unanswered when Theo called.

Gabby slipped quietly down the fire stairs and out into the lobby, crossed to the restaurant, and got a table by the windows. It was still snowing. There were no more than a half dozen of the white-clothed tables occupied. The breakfast buffet laid out on long banquet tables sat untouched and unwanted. Silverware gleamed on starched and creased napkins beside china place settings. Glasses gleamed beside crystal pitchers of orange and tomato juice. Even the centerpiece in the middle of the buffet table, a pineapple carved to look like a palm tree and surrounded by slices of fresh fruit, looked wilted and forlorn. Like it knew it was in the wrong place at the wrong time. The few people Gabby saw looked more concerned about getting the hell out of Dodge before the weather worsened than they did about having breakfast.

She ordered coffee and sat back to wait. It was barely five minutes before she saw Graham get off the elevator and stop at the desk before he went across the restaurant toward her. Gabby loved watching him, his movements, his long stride, the way his hips moved.

Graham smiled at Gabby as he approached the table. His eyes told Gabby what she already knew. He was as lost in her as she was in him. *And isn't that the pits,* she thought. *What the hell do we do now?*

"Gabby Franks, right?" Graham extended his hand, and Gabby took it. "Dr. Graham Wright. We met last night." There was a mischievous twinkle in his eyes.

"We certainly did, Dr. Wright," Gabby said softly.

"May I?" Graham pulled out the tapestry-covered chair next to Gabby.

"Please do."

CLOSE TO THE FLAME

"Quit talking like that, and quit looking at me like that," he whispered as he sat down. "Or we'll have to go back upstairs."

"Wonderful idea" Gabby's pulse raced at the thought. The musky smell of him filled her nostrils.

"You're the one who insisted on going to work." Graham dug in his pocket, pulled out the extra room key he'd gotten at the desk, then slipped it under the table to her. "In case you change your mind."

"It's Christmas. I'm in retailing. I have to go." Gabby took the key and slipped it in her jacket pocket. Just in case.

"I know." Graham sat back as the waitress poured their coffee.

"Buffet this morning?" the waitress asked him. She'd already tried to interest Gabby in it.

"Just coffee, thanks," Graham said. He waited until the tired-looking middle-aged woman moved away before he turned back to Gabby. "How late are you working?"

"I'll be off around six." *An eternity,* Gabby thought, *endless hours away from you. Oh no, what am I thinking? What are we doing? We can't honestly be making plans to continue this. Can we?*

"Buy you dinner?" Under the table, Graham's hand rested on Gabby's knee.

"What time's your lecture?"

"Eight again. Want to go?"

"Been there. Done that," Gabby teased. "But you're on for dinner."

"Good. And later?"

Gabby hesitated. "I need to be home."

"Phone call?" Gabby nodded. "I can miss this morning's by saying I had to run an errand or something. I can't miss them all."

"What are we going to do?"

Run like hell, went through Gabby's mind. *Get away from*

this man while you can. She tried. "This was supposed to be just a one-night stand," Gabby said. "Wasn't it?"

Graham shrugged. "Whatever it is, it isn't that."

"That's what *Cosmo* says, at least," Gabby continued. "What they call it. It's a phenomenon of the seventies. One-night stands." She knew she was babbling but was unable to stop herself. "It's the sexual revolution or something like that. You know, from all the old morality, all the old rules. New freedoms and all that. Free to be and do what you want to be and do."

"I wouldn't know," Graham said. His eyes on Gabby were amused. "I don't read *Cosmo.*"

"Well, according to them and what they say is etiquette, I should say thank you and walk away."

"Never happen."

"Not complicate our lives."

"You already have. We already have. Now, quit babbling and answer my question. What are we going to do?"

Gabby sighed and looked away from Graham. A determined woman in shoulder pads scurried past their table, obviously anxious to be somewhere else. Graham was right, and Gabby knew it. Walking away wasn't an option—hadn't been for almost twelve hours now.

"I'll come back after I get Theo's call," she said.

Graham smiled. "Weather looks nasty," he said when the waitress stopped at their table to leave the check.

"Airport's closed down," the waitress said matter-of-factly.

It was the truth of Boise winters. The airport closed when the fog rolled in this heavy, mixed with the snow, and blanketed the city in ice.

Gabby and Graham exchanged a secret hopeful look.

"How long? Are they saying?" he asked.

The waitress shrugged. "Got a blizzard predicted for tonight and tomorrow. More fog too. Who knows?" With practiced ease, she let the hot brown liquid lap the rims of their cups before she left to fill the other cups scattered sparsely around the room.

"Pray for lousy weather," Graham said softly.

"I already was," Gabby replied.

Gabby locked the big glass double doors of Lord and Young's as the last of the sixty daily employees, plus the twelve trainees, left. There were no customers to show out. It was not quite one o'clock on the replica of Big Ben inside the store's entryway. The snow was blowing sideways, lashing the window displays. Gabby imagined the elegantly dressed mannequins in the Christmas-decorated windows shivered and shrunk away from the storm's fury. Perversely, she considered throwing coats over them, then decided against it. Jack already thought she was one bubble short of plumb.

Turning back into the store and starting down the marbled aisles toward her office, Gabby saw Jack approaching from the direction of the boutique where she'd done her morning shopping. He wore a worried scowl across his tanned face.

"This is really lousy," Jack said as he neared Gabby. "Only days before Christmas, and we get a danged blizzard. Who can shop in a blizzard?"

"Nobody, Jack," Gabby told him in a voice filled with practiced patience. "That's why we're closing early, remember?"

The storm got worse as the day went on. At noon, the register readout told them they hadn't made enough to keep the lights on, much less pay the help and turn a profit. The small radio in Gabby's office urged everyone to get off the streets and stay there. The highway patrol had closed down Interstate 84, as well as all the roads leading into the Salmon River and Sawtooth Mountain Ranges. It happened every winter in Boise. Winter after winter, the lousy weather came, and every winter, Jack bitched.

"We do 50 percent of our business between Thanksgiving and Christmas," he said now. "Gabs, just look out there now." He motioned toward the doors where the snow was a blanket of white pulled down across the city.

"Jack, we're already 46 percent ahead of last year's figures,"

Gabby reminded him. "And 31 percent above plan. Quit griping."

Jack gave her a strange look. "What's the matter with you? Normally you're the last one to admit we need to close down. Today you seem anxious to get the hell out of here. Theo home, waiting for you?"

"Not hardly. He's in New York this week."

Jack raised an eyebrow. "Got a hot date?" He nodded toward the dress Gabby had bought that morning. It was a very short angora sweater-dress in winter white. It molded to her slender body and emphasized her shape. Together with the very high heels she had also bought, she looked incredible and knew it.

"Yeah, right." Gabby managed to laugh. "When do I have time?"

"Speaking of that..." Jack looked at the Rolex watch under the starched lavender cuff of his Dior shirt. "I need to call Barry. Let him know I have to stay downtown."

It was the opening Gabby had been waiting for. She tried to still her racing heart before she spoke. "Tell you what," she finally said as she linked her arm through Jack's and steered him toward the executive offices at the back of the store. "Since you have plans and I don't, since I don't even have Theo or the kids at home, I'll take the duty this time."

"You will, really?"

"I will, really."

Jack gave Gabby's cheek a kiss. "I'll owe you forever," he said.

"I know you will, and don't think I won't collect."

Jack gave her a grin and extricated his arm. "Then you won't mind if I just leave and let you take care of the details."

"Now who's in a hurry?"

"Me, I admit it," Jack said.

"Go ahead." Gabby laughed. "Have fun."

"I knew I'd never regret promoting you," Jack told Gabby

as he turned toward his office. "You make a wonderful vice president."

"Yeah, yeah," Gabby called after him. "And you make a wonderful boss. I'll be at the Hanover House if you need me."

"Just put everything on our account."

Don't worry, Gabby thought. *I plan to.*

She leaned back against a sparkling glass display case filled with designer perfumes, lotions, soaps, powders, and horribly expensive gift sets artistically arranged on Hermès scarves, and waited until Jack went to his office and got his overcoat, hat, and briefcase.

"I really appreciate this," he said, joining Gabby again. "Barry has his heart set on making this Christmas one I'll never forget."

"It's your first Christmas together," Gabby shrugged. "That's only natural."

"Yes, but does he have to bake different cookies and try a new recipe for mulled wine every night?"

"He loves you," Gabby said.

Jack actually blushed. "Don't let that get around."

"You know I won't."

"Yes. Yes, I do. Thank you, Gabs."

"Don't call me that. You know I hate it."

Jack laughed and planted another kiss on her cheek. "Yes. Okay, how's Mom?" he said, his brown eyes twinkling.

Jack, don't you even think it, let alone say it.

Gabby shooed him toward the doors, unlocked them, and let him out. Once he was on the sidewalk, buffeted by the wind and snow, clutching his tweed hat with its little red feather in its band tightly to his head, Gabby locked the heavy gilt-edged doors from the inside again. She went back through the spacious store with its entire Christmas splendor glowing brightly. Gabby turned out all but the nighttime security lights.

A hush descended over the usually busy store as the lights dimmed. To Gabby, it was a magical world now, a world that waited for the people to come back and make it real again. She loved the place when she was alone—the expensive merchandise, the impeccable displays, the dressed-to-kill mannequins. When she'd first gone to work at Dayton's at the tender age of twenty-one, a management trainee like the ones she escorted to the lecture last night, Gabby dreamed of someday being the person, the very important person, with the keys to this magical world.

So dreams do come true, Gabby thought, *at least some of them. Don't push your luck on the rest of this train of thought.* She heard her phone start ringing when she was about five feet from her office door and hurried to answer it. A priceless Aubusson carpet lay on her marbled floor; prints of the old masters lined her walls. Crystal lamps glowed on the top of her cherrywood antique desk. A spray of fresh roses sat on her credenza. She had them delivered twice weekly.

"Lord and Young's," she said in her best business voice as she picked the receiver up. "Gabby Franks speaking."

"My lecture's been canceled, Ms. Franks," Graham's sweet voice told her. "Because of the weather."

Immediately, Gabby felt a warm flush and sank down in her burgundy velvet Louis XIV chair. "I'm not surprised," she said. "I was just about to finish closing down the store. We've already sent everybody home and locked the doors."

The Waterford crystal clock on her desk read one fifteen.

"What are you planning to do?" Graham asked.

Gabby could almost hear him hold his breath while he waited for her answer. It made her dizzy with needing him.

"Either Jack or I stay downtown when this happens," she said. Her voice was soft and sensual and meant to promise Graham all his fantasies would come true. "In case of emergency or alarm failures or whatever. So there's someone who can get to the store."

"Who's staying this time?"

Graham tried to sound casual when he asked that. He didn't, and Gabby smiled.

"I am," she said softly. "I volunteered. Guess where we always stay?"

"Where?"

"Hanover House."

"Fate," Graham said the word softly again.

"I did some more shopping, picked up a few things to see me through. Just in case Jack fell for my little trick. I have to ring out the registers, total the figures, put them in the book, set the alarm." There was the briefest pause. "Then I'm on my way."

"How long?" It was a husky whisper that sent lovely shivers down Gabby's spine.

"Thirty minutes or less if I run the red lights?"

"Too long."

"I'll hurry. Then when I get there, I'll check in then come to your room."

The mists were swirling around Gabby again. The ancients were beckoning. She closed her eyes and let them carry her away, back to Graham's waiting arms, and more, so much more.

"Did you make a reservation?"

"I will as soon as we hang up. For the room next to yours."

"There's a connecting door."

"I know," Gabby whispered. "I planned it that way."

"Hurry. I'll unlock the door on this side."

Gabby walked past Graham's door without so much as a glance in its direction. She could picture him sitting there, waiting for her, and her pulse raced. *Keep this up and you're going to have a damned heart attack,* she warned herself.

Outside, she remained the picture of calm and poise as the young bellhop opened her door and held it for her. He put the small overnight bag she'd bought when she picked up the things she needed to tide her over on the foldout luggage rack, then waited for his tip.

Gabby gave him five dollars, pleased at the look on his face. It was Christmas, after all. And his tips would be suffering from the weather just like everybody's in the large old hotel.

Once the bellhop closed the door to her room, Gabby took off her jacket and hung it over the back of a chair, set her briefcase beside the bed, then walked softly across the plush carpeting and turned the handle on the door connecting her room to Graham's. It made a soft click as she opened it.

"Miss me?" she asked, as she stood in the doorway lit from behind. She saw the unmistakable passion on Graham's face and hurried to close the distance between them. The soft dress she wore was so short, the length of her legs flashed out.

Graham couldn't take his eyes off her.

"Missed you incredibly," he said.

Before the words were barely out of his mouth, Gabby was in his arms, and he was laughing and kissing her. Gabby molded her body to his and willed the kiss to never end. It did, finally, and when it did, she caught her breath and looked up at Graham solemnly.

"It's just the passion," she said. "Please tell me that's the only reason I can't stay away from you."

Graham's look was equally sober. "I can't do that," he said.

"It's got to be," Gabby said. "We have no future anyplace else. No right to claim anything beyond this."

"If it's just that, why did I feel so lost and alone after you left me this morning?"

"We can't do this, Graham," she whispered against his chest. "We can't let it grow into anything but a brief affair. It's got to be over when the weather clears and you go back to California."

"That's what my mind says too. My soul and every fiber of my being keep trying to tell it to my heart."

"Did it, or should I ask, will it listen?"

"Not a chance."

Gabby sighed. She was in the circle of his arms, safe and warm. *Where I belong,* she thought. "I know. Mine won't either. And I've tried. I really have."

"Me too. I have no idea what you've done to me, lady. Woven

some kind of spell, some kind of magic, some kind of witchcraft around me is all I can figure."

Gabby rested her head against Graham's chest and inhaled deeply. His scent was so masculine and filled with a clean, intoxicating aroma. "Maybe I'm just your midlife crisis."

Graham's sudden, spontaneous laughter filled the room.

"What's so funny?" Gabby asked.

"That you should come up with that term."

"Why?"

"Because on the way to the airport yesterday, I used it myself. When I told myself to shape up and quit wanting more than I had. Or maybe I should say—when I tried to convince myself that what I had was what I wanted."

"So it's at least a contingency?" Gabby said hopefully. After all, one of them needed to keep their senses about them. And it sure didn't look like it was going to be her.

Graham traced the contours of Gabby's face with his hand. "I'm afraid it's not," he told her. "I think of you more as one of life's infinite possibilities."

"Infinite possibilities," she repeated.

"Something I thought I'd never find again, something that seemed beyond my reach, and something I thought I'd forfeited forever."

"That's a little more serious than a midlife crisis, isn't it?"

Graham laughed again. "You could say that." He traced Gabby's features with one gentle finger. "I tried this morning after you left to figure out what was going on between us. And what the hell I was going to do about it."

He looked down at Gabby with the green eyes she hadn't been able to get out of her mind all day. "I had no answer then, and I don't have one now," he said. "All I know is that in less than twenty-four hours, you've become an obsession with me, Ms. Franks. I want you with me, in my sight and within touching distance all the time. When you walk out of a room, you take all the light with you. You take all my senses and my heart with you."

"That sounds like something I should apologize for."

"Don't you dare." Graham let his hand fall down to her waist.

"This isn't like me, Gabby. I've always been able to walk away from anything. Today I felt something was pulling me in too deep, something threatening, maybe even dangerous, anything outside my carefully constructed life plan. But I don't seem to be able to walk away from this. I know, beyond the shadow of a doubt, I am definitely getting in way too deep here. I'm over my head in places I've never been before. Gabby, I also know I should run like hell."

"But you're still here." Gabby felt her body responding to Graham and almost wished they hadn't started this conversation. She wanted reassurances from him. She wanted him to tell her, yes, it was just passion, and they'd part when he had to go home, and it would all be over. What she didn't want was to find out he was feeling as vulnerable and unsettled as she was.

"I'm still here," he said. "I couldn't leave even if I wanted to. California is a lifetime away. Patti is a lifetime away. They have no reality to me, no hold over me. Right now, only one thing matters. And that's you."

Graham stopped after he said that, his eyes on Gabby so intense she was sure he could see all the way to her soul and read what was written there. "So what are we going to do?"

A knock on his door was her answer. Gabby jumped like she'd been caught with her hand in the safe at work, extricating hundred-dollar bills.

"Relax," Graham said, letting her go reluctantly. "It's only room service."

"I'll go to my room until he's gone." Gabby was already halfway there before the words were out of her mouth.

"Hurry back," Graham said as he went to answer the door.

He waited just briefly until he heard the latch on the connecting door catch, then swung his door open.

"Hey there," he said to the man from room service.

"Good afternoon, sir."

A stooped, gray-haired man in an impeccably starched white jacket moved into the room, pushing a small service cart containing a silver ice bucket with a bottle protruding out of it. Next to the silver bucket sat two tulip glasses. The man extricated the bottle and showed Graham its label.

Graham nodded. "Fine," he said, signing his name on the check and tipping the man.

As soon as the door to his room was pulled closed, Graham went to the bedside table and pulled open its drawer. Before he gave Gabby the all clear, he placed a small box wrapped in silver paper and tied with red ribbon beside the champagne.

At the connecting door, he knocked once. "Come out, come out, wherever you are."

Gabby opened the door immediately. "I'm right here," she said. "Don't shout."

"I didn't shout."

"Sounded like a shout."

"Only because you had your ear to the door, listening in."

Gabby felt a warm flush start up her face. "You're right." She laughed. "I did."

"I knew it," Graham said.

"How did you know it?"

"Because I've already come to a conclusion about you. You can't stand the thought of missing even a minute of what's going on, can you?"

It was such a spot of truth, such a strong insight into her personality, that it spooked Gabby. "Oh god," she said. "Don't figure me out. Please. Don't start reading my mind."

"Why not? You read mine. Besides, are you afraid of what I'll see in there?"

Yes, Gabby thought. *I'm afraid you'll see that I'm scared to death I'm falling in love with you, Graham Wright.* "Not hardly," was what she said, "just a lot of empty space holding my ears apart."

"Yeah right." Graham laughed. "Tell me another bedtime story." Gabby decided the safest course of action was changing the subject, so she did. "What's all this?" She nodded to the bottle chilling in its silver ice bucket.

"Champagne."

Gabby walked over to the table. "Nice. Are we celebrating something?" She spied the small box and picked it up. "Since when did room service deliver small boxes tied with red ribbon?"

"Something for you," Graham said as he came up behind her and took her in his arms.

"Now or later?" she asked.

Graham took a ragged breath. "Later."

Then he whispered, "Elegant. That's what you are, completely elegant."

Her expensive perfume floated across the space between them as Gabby moved away.

"I've never known anyone like you," Graham whispered. "Never."

"There is nothing else like me," Gabby said softly. "I'm an enigma in search of a paradox."

"Then just call me paradox," Graham said.

Gabby tangled her hands in his curls and pressed him against her.

Graham was gentle, tender, and thoughtful as a lover. He also loved Gabby like she'd never been loved before. His heart, his soul, as well as his body, made love to her. He pleased her, devoured her, and drove her to heights she didn't believe possible and never suspected existed.

Afterward, he poured champagne into the tulip glasses and handed one to her. "To loving you," he said.

"And to you, Graham. You who does it so well," Gabby

whispered. She raised her glass. "And to whatever time we have together."

"Let's not talk about that. Let's not talk about endings yet. In fact, let's not talk about pasts or futures, either. For once in my life, I want to live in the present and think no further than right this minute. This minute with you." Graham handed her the small box.

"Now?" she asked.

"Now," he replied.

With shaking hands, Gabby pulled the ribbon off and opened the box. She wasn't used to presents for no reason at all. A velvet box from the jeweler's in the lobby of the hotel sat inside.

"What in the world?" She looked up at Graham, and what she saw in his eyes tore holes in the careful composure of her life.

"Open it and see."

In the small velvet box, nestled against peach satin, was a delicate pair of perfectly matched pearls. "They're beautiful," Gabby breathed, touching them with reverent hands. "So very beautiful."

"Put them on."

Gabby took the gold knots she wore in her ears out then replaced them with the pearls. She held the curtain of hair back so Graham could see them. "I'll never take them off," she whispered, tears in her eyes. "I'll wear them forever."

"Forever?"

"Forever," Gabby promised.

The word *forever* hung suspended between them as Graham took her in his arms again.

Tennessee
December 30, 1993

"People don't die from broken hearts," a jaded and worldly friend had once remarked to Gabby.

"Not all at once," Gabby had answered quietly. "They do it a little bit at a time. Day after day, year after year."

Annie strained toward the door, determined to get back to the warmth of the fire. "You're a wimp," Gabby told her. She opened the heavy front door and let the dog inside then unsnapped her leash.

Theo looked up when the dog got to the living room. "You're all wet," he said. Annie wagged then shook herself, scattering water droplets in a spray around her.

"It's snowing, Theo." Gabby took off her jacket, hung it in the foyer closet, stepped out of her wet shoes, then continued down the long hall.

Once in the downstairs bathroom, she got a towel and carried it back to dry the dog. The face that stared back at her from the mirror over the console table in the hall wore a haunted look she was all too familiar with.

"Did you pick up the cleaning today?" Theo was holding the dog away from him, keeping her at arm's length until Gabby rescued him.

"Of course, Theo." Gabby retrieved the dog, dried her shiny coat, and then shooed her toward the fire.

"I need the new suit next week. That's the only reason I asked."

Gabby was on her way back to the bathroom and the hamper with the wet towel. "It's in your closet," she called back.

"Got anything planned for tomorrow night?"

Gabby dropped the towel in on top of the dirty dishcloths and towels from downstairs then started back toward the living room. Tomorrow night was New Year's Eve. "No," she called.

God, no, she silently added.

Theo was used to Gabby's aversion to doing things over the holidays. It never bothered him. He was uncomfortable in social situations anyway, and Gabby offered him the perfect out.

"Talk to any of the kids this week?"

"All of them," Gabby said, appearing in the french doors to the living room. She went to her favorite chair and sat down.

"Charlie said, 'I love you, Grandma.'"

"He did?"

Gabby nodded, smiling softly, as she thought about the children. Theo, with his husband's duty dispatched, went back to his reading.

I wish you knew them, Graham. When anybody asks me what I accomplished in this life, I don't think of the career that filled me for so long, of the years of glamour working for Jack, of the important people I knew, of the promotions and the money and the freedoms. Instead, I point to my children with unabashed pride.

I wish I could also tell the world that, in my life, you, Graham, loved me. I would like you to know how all the children have grown and what they have become in their life.

My oldest daughter Sarah's an engineer and will be thirty this year. She and her husband have a four-year-old little girl they call Danny and another baby due this spring.

Sue is twenty-eight. She has a little boy, BJ, who's seven. Her new husband, a widower, has a little girl the same age. They just bought an old house they're redoing over in Oak Ridge.

Sam is twenty-six. She's a chef, Cordon Bleu trained, in one of Atlanta's fanciest restaurants. Still unmarried, though she and Matt have been a couple for years now. She says she won't marry. If

Matt is in a bad mood now, she can send him home. If she marries him, she has to put up with it. Sam would've been much happier living in the sixties.

Jay is twenty-five. He's an instructor at the Combined Armed Forces Intelligence School and has a little boy, not quite three, called Charlie. I once made the mistake of asking him what they taught at intelligence school. He said if he told me, he'd have to kill me. Ring a bell? I didn't ask again. Unlike me, I'm not sure he was joking.

She was brought back to the reality of today as Theo spoke.

"Want a drink?" Theo asked, standing in front of her.

"You know what I'd really like?" Gabby said without thinking. "A margarita."

Theo gave her a strange look. "You haven't had one of those in twenty years."

"Seventeen," she corrected him, again without thinking.

"Seventeen years."

"Do we have the stuff to make one?"

"No." Gabby realized her slipup and recovered quickly.

Actually, she did have the makings for her margaritas, but that was for later. "It was just an aberrant thought, Theo. Whatever you're having is fine."

Later, when they'd finished their drinks and Theo went up to bed, Gabby took the pins out of her heavy hair and let it fall to her shoulders. She still wore it long for Graham because that was the way he'd liked it.

She stared at the fire, the old pearls glistening in her ears. So much of her life was lived the way Graham would have liked her to live it. So much was said and done with him in mind. So much of the goodness and patience inside her came from loving him and being loved by him. Like she thought, somehow, he'd know.

Boise
Friday, December 23, 1976

You could say it's till death do us part because I'll surely
die when you leave. At least, the best part of me will.

"The airport's shut down, Theo. I don't know if I can get out." Gabby stood beside the couch in Graham's room and twisted the phone cord around her slender fingers as she talked.

Graham stood behind her, his arms around her waist and his lips buried in her hair.

"They don't know yet," she continued. "I think the best solution is for you to fly to Minneapolis like you'd planned. At least, that way, the kids will have one parent there."

Gabby paused and listened to the disappointment on the other end. "You know I'll be there if they open the airport. And I can get a flight."

She leaned back against Graham and felt him breathe deeply, inhaling her fragrance, she knew.

"If I have to spend Christmas alone, I have to spend Christmas alone, Theo. I'll live through it, OK? At least I'm in the hotel instead of home alone. I won't be tempted to eat carrot sticks and call it Christmas dinner."

Graham leaned around and kissed Gabby's cheek. His hands moved up to cradle her in his arms. Gabby barely kept her concentration. "I was supposed to fly out tomorrow afternoon and back the next afternoon. If I can't get out tomorrow, there's no sense in coming. I'd have to fly in and out the same day." She looked down and saw Graham's large, beautiful hands.

"No, Theo. You were scheduled to fly back to wherever you need to be next week, and the kids won't fly back until New Year's Day or the day after."

Graham kissed the hollow of her throat, and Gabby almost lost her train of thought. She struggled back to her conversation.

"Don't worry about me. I'm a big girl. I'll be fine."

Gabby's voice softened. "It's one Christmas, Theo. We have the rest of our lives to make up for it." Implicit in her words was the understanding she and Graham didn't. She and Graham had only this one Christmas, and they only had it if the weather stayed socked in—*if, please, Lord,* she silently prayed.

At length, she said good-bye and hung the phone up gently. "Your turn."

Graham took a deep breath and blew it out before he nodded in the direction of the phone. "I should have it that easy," he said.

"I can leave if you like."

"Don't you dare."

Gabby smiled and let him pull her down on the couch beside him.

"Hey," he said when the number was dialed and the connection made. "What are you up to?" Gabby could hear faint wisps of a feminine voice as it answered him. "You've heard. Patti, I don't know what to tell you. The odds on getting out of here aren't good, that's all." Graham played with Gabby's fingers as he talked. "I thought maybe you'd like to fly in and see your folks."

Gabby reached over and lightly stroked his skin. The reaction was instantaneous. Graham looked at her with eyes suddenly blind and full of love.

"Well, why don't you stay next week too," he managed to say. "I'm going to have to skip Christmas and fly straight to the seminar from here, it looks like."

Gabby sat down on his lap and began to nuzzle his neck.

"Oh yes." Graham mouthed the words to Gabby as he wrapped

his free hand in her silky hair. Aloud to Patti he said, "I thought so. You haven't seen them in quite a while."

Gabby watched Graham's eyes close and heard his breath catch as she moved her head slowly around his neck and earlobes.

"What?" he said. "No, no, there's nothing wrong with my voice. Just a little hoarse from the damnable weather." Graham cleared the huskiness out of his throat with a great deal of effort before he continued. He didn't make any effort at all to stop what Gabby was doing. "Make the arrangements, call, and let me know what they are. If by some fluke, the airport gets back in business, I'll fly to your folks' tomorrow instead of home."

"What seminar?" Gabby asked after he hung up. She was still on his lap, her hand fondling his chest with infinite tenderness.

"The Ethics Roundtable. In Rum Springs."

"Is it open to anyone?" She leaned over and kissed him.

In spite of what she was doing, Graham somehow managed to follow her line of thought.

"Yes. There are representatives from every field of business and academia flying in."

"I think," Gabby said softly, "it's something Jack needs to send me to." She was working lazy circles around his skin.

"Will he?" Graham asked.

Gabby raised her head. "Of course. I'll just have to threaten him a little."

"Do it," he said.

"Do what?" she asked. Her eyes twinkled, and her soul loved the reaction she was getting from Graham. She leaned over and kissed him again.

"Call first," he said. "But hurry."

"I'll be back," she promised. To emphasize her words, Gabby gave him a last lingering kiss.

She grabbed the phone off the end table, sat cross-legged on the floor, and called Jack. Graham's eyes were glued to her.

"I can't tell you why I need to go, Jack. Don't ask. Yes, it does have something to do with being the one to volunteer to stay downtown." Gabby closed her eyes when Graham leaned over and ran his fingers gently up her body. "If I tell you that, I'll have to kill you."

Graham grinned, almost laughed out loud, and Gabby put a hand up to silence him.

"All right. I'll owe you forever and a day instead of the other way around," she finally said. Her breath was coming in short little gasps. "And it'll stay our little secret?"

Gabby waited, eyes closed, for Jack's answer. "Then yes, it involves a man. That's all I'm saying, Jack. All I'll ever say. Now, are you happy?"

Gabby broke the connection blindly without saying good-bye; she handed Graham the phone.

"Devil," she said shakily. "You did that on purpose."

"I'm sorry," Graham answered. "I couldn't stop."

Gabby shook her head and smiled at him. "You're not sorry. Not even a little bit. You enjoyed it. Don't lie."

"You're right. I'm not. But I am telling the truth about not being able to stop."

"That I believe." Her hand brushed him lightly. "Make my flight reservations, will you? Same flight you're taking." Graham made her reservations while she sat at his feet and watched. She was gently caressing him again. He fondled her hair, her shoulder, anything he could reach.

Mission accomplished, Graham handed the phone back, and Gabby hung it up.

"Now," he said. "Can we take up where we left off earlier? Please?"

"You mean this?" She pulled him close for a full kiss. She lowered her full, warm body on his lap again. He wrapped his hands in her hair and pressed her close to him.

Gabby closed her eyes and felt the world float away.

Tennessee
December 30, 1993

Eleven and a half months a year, Gabby is the perfect wife.
Something happens to her around Christmas and New Year's.
Some kind of sadness she gets lost in.
"Too many years in retailing," she says.
I think it's just what the shrinks call seasonal blues.
—Theo Franks

Gabby stoked the fire until it glowed brightly again. The house was dark and quiet. Annie was asleep on the couch. Upstairs, Theo would be under his mound of covers and snoring by now.

Silently, Gabby went into the large downstairs room she used as a studio. Her drafting table, her easel, her desk with its brand-new computer, her pencils, paints, brushes, and books imparted her distinctive personality to the large room. There were bookcases on all four walls, all filled to overflowing with books. A Navajo rug in white, blue, and terra-cotta rested on the polished floor. Her paintings hung on the walls and were stacked in all the room's corners. A white futon rested against one wall, in front of a bookcase.

It was Gabby's space, all hers, her private world, and a gift from Theo for moving to Tennessee with him.

Gabby lifted the top on the battered wooden paint box on her worktable and carefully removed the crumpled tubes of paint. There were dozens and dozens of them, color-flecked and messy. She stacked them neatly on the drafting table. Next, she lifted the false wooden bottom of the box.

From beneath it she took a sketch, timeworn and beginning to fade. It was a watercolor she did when she first got back from Rum Springs. Her one remembrance, the one piece of evidence she was never able to destroy.

Graham's face smiled out at her, blue skies behind him and white snows around him. It was the smile he had just for her. His lean, hard body was a sharp contrast to his soft and gentle eyes.

If Gabby laid her fingertip on his full lips, she could feel his tender kiss even now, in this house on this silent and lonely night. If she touched the curls, she could remember the texture of them under her fingers.

She held the sketch in her hands and let all the old feelings wash over her. Once a year, she permitted this self-indulgence. Once a year, she allowed herself to take out this remembrance she painted with all the love in her heart and stare into Graham's bottomless green eyes again.

Once a year, she wondered about the "might have been." She was only human. That much was allowed her.

Boise
Saturday, December 24, 1976

Roses For Gabby

There is one Christmas in my life I'll remember always and never be able to share with anyone. One I'll measure every other Christmas by. One that will forever live only in my soul.

"It's Christmas Eve," Graham whispered softly.

"Not until tonight." Gabby snuggled her morning-warm body into the safe curve of his arm and closed her eyes again.

"It's the twenty-fourth all day." Graham laughed. "Not just tonight." His hand stroked her hair gently.

"But it's not Christmas Eve until tonight. Trust me. I'm the one with all the kids. It's not Christmas Eve until dark. It took me a long time to convince the monsters of that."

"All the kids," Graham said softly and so wistfully that Gabby picked up on it immediately. Funny, he'd seemed almost resigned to it when they first talked about her kids.

She rose up on one elbow and looked at him. "You miss having children, don't you, Graham?"

He sat up on the side of the bed. If he smoked cigarettes, now would be the time he lit one. "Yes. Yes, I do."

Gabby could sense he wanted to say more, so she lay there quietly and waited for him to continue. At length, he did.

"Family," he said. "It's very important to me, Gabby. It always was. And I always assumed I'd have one. Took it for granted, I guess. I mean, that's what two people in love do, isn't it? Get married then have children?"

"Most people, yes," Gabby said. "Some even do it the other way around, but it's not really recommended."

That got her the slight smile she'd hoped for before Graham spoke again. "It's such a void," he said. "Something feels so incomplete in your life when you don't have the family you've always wanted. When there are no little ones binding the two of you together, it's not the same. You tend to drift off in different directions."

"Then why..." Gabby let the sentence die. She really couldn't understand the conscious choice not to have children. Like Graham, it had always seemed the most natural thing in the world to her.

It took Graham a while to answer her again, and when he did, it was with one word. "Patti," he finally said. Brief, succinct.

"What about Patti?"

"She wants a career in show business."

"I know that," Gabby said. "But my lord, what's that got to do with anything? I'm not in show business, granted, or trying to be. But it can't be that much different or more demanding than retailing. I mean, I have a career, a husband, and four kids."

Graham looked back across his shoulder at her. "I know," he answered softly. "I know."

"And?"

Graham looked down at his clasped hands. "Let's just say that knowing you has opened my eyes to certain things—you, your career, your sense of family, your children, your love of life, and your sense of humor. The fact that you manage to balance all that, be all that, do all that, and do it so damned successfully." He looked off into space again before he continued. "I guess I feel cheated, Gabby. Cheated and terribly jealous of Theo because he has everything I want. It's made me see there is a large degree of selfishness in Patti's life. She says it's her decision."

Secretly, Gabby agreed with Graham about Patti's refusal to have children. But she was damned if she would make any derogatory remarks about his wife. It would make her feel too much like the typical other woman. Instead she said, "Maybe she's frightened, Graham."

"Afraid of a baby, a small child? Good Lord, give me a break."

"She's young. You said so yourself."

"How old were you?"

"When the first one was born?"

Graham nodded.

Gabby sighed. "Twenty-one," she admitted.

"Patti is way over twenty-one," Graham said.

"Twenty-seven. I know. You told me," Gabby said. "But I was a very mature twenty-one. Maybe Patti is a very immature twenty-seven."

Graham just looked at her.

"Okay," Gabby said, searching her mind for something good to say. "Maybe she's afraid of losing her looks? Since she wants to be an actress." She almost added *when she grows up* but had to bite her tongue to hold it back.

Graham looked across the bed at Gabby, and a little bit of the twinkle was back in his eyes. "Like you lost yours, you mean?"

"That better be a joke, pardner," Gabby warned him.

"You know it is," he said.

"You're right." She smiled. "I do."

"Of course you do. So why do you know me so much better in two days than Patti does in six years?" he asked quietly. "Can you tell me that?"

Gabby looked down at the bed and smoothed out an imaginary wrinkle. "Is that her fault, Graham? Or yours?"

Graham got up and walked over to the small bar in the corner of the room. He opened the tiny refrigerator, took out a can of Diet Coke, popped its tab, and took a long swallow before he looked back at Gabby. "I suppose you want an honest answer."

Gabby nodded.

Graham walked back to the bed and sat down. He offered the Coke to Gabby. She took a swallow then handed it back to him.

"A little of both, I think, maybe a lot of both. I don't know how it happened, but I seem to walk on eggshells around Patti. Not bring up subjects I know are going to cause another of her tearful fits. Her wounded-bird routine." He wiped the condensation off the can with a corner of the spread then set the Coke down on the bedside table. "You know, 'If you loved me, you wouldn't be doing this'? So I guess it's both our faults. Hers for being that way, mine for accepting it."

"Same here," Gabby said.

"Theo?"

Again, Gabby nodded. "Not tearful fits, of course. Just an unspoken agreement between us that I will keep his life structured and uncomplicated. Be his buffer to the world, if you will. For that reason, I don't let Theo see the side of me he doesn't want to see." She looked back across the bed at Graham and smiled gently. "You know, I didn't even realize I did that until I met you. Didn't realize how hard I try to be exactly the person Theo needs to believe he's sharing his life with."

"And is he sharing his life with you, Gabby? I mean, really?"

This time, a sad resignation filled Gabby's eyes. "As well as he can, Graham. As well as he knows how, and to the full extent of his abilities to be intimate with another person. He gives me all he can."

"Is that enough?"

"It has to be."

"And I'll bet even that's contingent on your keeping your part of the bargain. On your staying the person he thinks he married."

"Something like that, yeah. Theo has a very hard time sharing himself, you see. And that's made me quit sharing myself with him." There was a long pause while Gabby watched the snow falling outside the balcony doors. "I guess I spend an awful lot of time and effort being what and who Theo thinks I am."

"But you aren't really?"

"It's who I thought I was until this, until you. Now I see

how much more I am with you than I ever was or ever will be with Theo."

"What do you mean?"

"How can I explain it?" Gabby looked back at Graham, at his serious and gentle face, at the deep-green pools of his eyes, at his sensuous mouth. She wanted to boil her feelings down to their simplest parts, somehow let him know how much he meant to her, how much this time spent with him, this stolen time, meant to her. "I'm myself with you, Graham," she finally said. "Nothing more, nothing less. And that's enough for you. I can laugh with you, joke with you, and not always be so deadly serious. Do you know how nice that is that you have no preconceived ideas of who I should be? What I should be?"

"And Theo obviously does."

"Theo wants perfection in his world. One and one are always two. B always comes after A." Gabby's voice was both sad and resigned as she put this into words.

"So you pretend to be perfect for him?"

"Let's say I don't rock his boat, that's all."

"Maybe you should."

"No. Theo was like this when I married him. After the first year or so, I realized I couldn't change him, Graham. But at the same time, I realized Theo was a good husband, a good father, and a good provider. A good man. Someone with whom I could share a comfortable life."

"Comfortable."

"Comfortable, and I decided to settle for that. After all, it was more than a whole lot of people had, and I never was one of those girls who waited for someone to come along and sweep them off their feet. The decision to marry Theo was always based more on logic than emotion."

"And you don't regret that?"

"It's been a good decision," Gabby said, not really answering him. "It's worked for us."

"Then why this?" Graham asked her softly. "Why me?"

It took Gabby a long time to answer that. She sat very still, weighing her words, not wanting to lead them into territory she knew they should avoid, had to avoid if they were going to walk away from this with any semblance of their sanity.

"Because," she finally said, "when I least expected it, someone did come along and sweep me off my feet. Someone who made me feel all the things I gave up feeling when I married Theo. Someone who brought back all my girlhood dreams of Prince Charming. Someone who made me believe in love again. You came along, Graham. And changed my world."

"I'm not a Prince Charming, Gabby," Graham said.

"I know you aren't. But you are real and caring and willing to share all of yourself with me. Not just little bits and pieces."

"Like Theo."

"Ah, God. He tries, Graham. He really does."

"And so do I with Patti. But in my heart I know I do the same thing Theo does. I give her those same little bits and pieces, just enough to hold off her tirades, just enough to keep the peace."

"Do you really?"

It was Graham's time to nod. "I give her what she wants too, Gabby. Just like you give Theo what he wants. Until I met you, until I knew what it was like to share myself completely and openly and honestly with another person, I didn't know that wasn't enough. For either one of us."

"Neither did I," Gabby said. "Neither did I, Graham."

"But now that I do—"

"Don't, Graham. Please. Don't go there."

He stopped talking and just watched her. The silence built around them, alive and expectant. Gabby knew she was afraid to take the discussion any further and hoped her words had stopped Graham from doing the same. There were dangers, very serious dangers, lurking out of sight in the thoughts and feelings she was trying so hard to avoid.

After what seemed an eternity to Gabby, Graham finally spoke. Evidently, he picked up on her warning, because he changed the subject. "I know you like walking in the snow. How about walking in the rain?"

"Love it." Gabby smiled. "So do you, right?"

"You're reading my mind again, but yes, I do. And rainy afternoons should be spent in bed with someone you love."

"Eating Chinese food out of paper cartons and working crossword puzzles in pen."

"Exactly," Graham said.

"Soul mates," Gabby told him in a tone that was meant to be light.

"Meant to be," Graham answered. "No. No, Gabby." He took a deep breath and used his eyes to bore into her very soul. "What should have been, what should be, what could be."

That comment, so softly said, scared Gabby into changing the subject herself this time. "Do you like camping?" she asked.

Graham allowed himself to be led away from the precipice they were tottering on. "Love it."

"The mountains?"

"And coffee over a campfire on cold, clear mornings. Smoke drifting over a still lake, the cry of a loon, and the smell of bacon on the wind."

"Snuggling in a sleeping bag together all night."

"Then going fishing."

Gabby sighed. "Yes. Like that."

Graham stretched back down beside Gabby. "Theo doesn't, does he?"

"Theo's idea of roughing it is no room service," Gabby said dryly.

"Then he and Patti would make a great pair. Think we should introduce them?"

"Naw," Gabby said. "Much too early. Maybe later on."

She wrapped one long leg over Graham's body, turning in to him, and felt the old stirrings again.

"Miss the kids?" Graham asked as he ran his hand down her back.

"Of course. They're my children. They're a big part of my life, Graham. I also miss Theo. But this is only one Christmas, and I'll never have another one like it." Gabby pulled herself up into bed with him.

"The airport may be open." Graham took her in his arms as he teased her.

"The gods can't be that cruel," Gabby whispered.

She was right. They weren't. The blizzard continued all day, made worse by the fog. They had room service in her room, never dressed, never ventured out.

Gabby talked to Theo and the kids, wished her parents "Merry Christmas," and promised to go see them in the spring. She told Theo about the seminar Jack decided to send her to and promised him she'd be back next Friday.

When the phone in Graham's room rang, he tumbled out of Gabby's bed in a mass of tangled covers and talked to Patti. He wished her parents "Merry Christmas" and then promised to see them in the spring. He told Patti he'd be home from the seminar Friday.

"Parallel lives," Gabby said softly. She sipped at a glass of champagne Graham brought back with him. She was suddenly solemn and introspective.

"What do you mean?" Graham dunked a bright-red strawberry in his glass then fed it to her.

"I'll go home. You'll go home. I'll fly to see my folks as if nothing's changed. You'll fly to see Patti's as if nothing's changed."

Graham wiped a smear of strawberry juice off her chin with his fingers. The drop that fell on her breast, he licked away.

"It doesn't have to be that way," he said quietly, almost experimentally, like he was trying the words on for size. He watched her closely the whole time. "We don't have to let this end, Gabby, not now, not ever."

Gabby just looked at him, her pulse suddenly racing. *Well, damn*, she thought. *Now he's done it. Done what I've tried so hard not to do. He's taken the step we shouldn't have taken. Gone where we have no business going. And, dear Lord, I want to go with him.* This realization tore at Gabby's heart, and she kept her tone as breezy as possible when she answered him. "Sure it does, Graham. It has to be that way because of who we are."

"It's the seventies. Divorce isn't a dirty word anymore."

"Isn't it? You going to tell Theo that? Tell Patti that? Tell my kids that? If push really came to shove, I don't believe either of us can purposely hurt six innocent people."

"The alternative scares me more than that does."

"And what's the alternative?"

"Life without you."

Gabby got up fully, consciously nude and walked across the room to stare out the doors at her balcony. Snow was banked halfway up them and swirled against the glass. Her breath made delicate fog patterns where it touched the cold surface.

"How did we get in so deep so fast, Graham?" she asked quietly.

He sat up on the edge of the bed again. "I'm not sure," he said. "I think it has a lot to do with this."

"What?"

"Being able to talk to you. Tell you things I've never told another person. It's like I've found the other half of myself with you, Gabby. I know what you're thinking before you say it. What you're going to do before you do it. What you want before you tell me. You do the same with me."

"That's because we're so much alike, because we want the same things and need the same things."

"Dream the same dreams. Yes. Yes, we do, Gabby. Plus, you've touched me on a level I didn't even know I had. At least, not anymore."

"And what level is that?"

He couldn't help grinning as he did a Groucho Marx take of Gabby's nude body. "You mean besides the obvious?"

Gabby laughed. "Besides that."

"I guess you've shown me that the boundaries and limitations I set for myself, as well as accepted in others, can be overcome, can be surpassed. And that there are depths of feeling I had buried. Things I want and had given up hope of getting. With you, Gabby, it seems like all things are possible."

"With the love of a good woman, you mean?" she tried to joke.

Suddenly, Graham was deadly serious. "Do I have that?" he asked her.

Gabby stared across the abyss of the room at him. *The hell with it,* she thought. *Go on, risk it, and go there with him, at least for a while. You'll never have another chance like this.* "Yes," she said in the softest of voices. "Yes. Heaven help us both, but I'm afraid you do."

Gabby realized he'd been holding his breath, waiting for her answer, when she heard him expel it.

"Don't make it sound so sad," he said. "It isn't. It's wonderful. To find this..."

"Maybe I'm afraid to love you, Graham."

"Afraid? Why?"

"Because of what it's doing to me."

"It's making me happier than I've ever been in my life. What's it doing to you, Gabby?"

"Changing me. Do you know what being with you is like for me? Always safe, always sane—Gabby Franks?"

"What?"

"Let me start by telling you what it's not like." Gabby turned her back on Graham and stared out at the world of white beyond the glass doors. "Being with Theo is like floating down a river on a lazy summer afternoon in one of those big, safe inner tubes. No, not a river—a stream, a creek, someplace where my feet touch the bottom all the time and I know exactly what's around the next curve. Exactly what to expect."

Graham waited silently for her to continue.

When Gabby turned back to look at Graham, there were tears

in her eyes. No one was more surprised than she was. "Being with you is like being in the middle of the damned ocean in the middle of a damned storm with nothing to keep me afloat but a waterlogged piece of old driftwood. It's deep and dangerous. It's highly charged and emotional. And I don't know what's going to happen because I've never been there before. The currents may sweep me away and drown me. The feelings may consume me." Her voice grew even softer. "It's the most exciting and wonderful and intense thing I've ever known, Graham. But it's also the scariest."

"Why is it so scary? Love shouldn't be scary."

"But it is," Gabby whispered. "I have this horrible feeling the ocean is going to chew me up into little pieces and spit me out on some deserted beach and I'll never ever be able to fit the pieces back together again." The tears that had pooled in her eyes like a banked-up stream suddenly overflowed. "Loving you may destroy me, Graham. At the very least, I know it'll change my life forever. I won't walk away from this the same person who walked into it. I'll never be that person again."

"And that scares you?"

"Of course it does. I knew that person so well. She had her life all planned and under perfect control—no surprises, no highs, no lows, steady and even."

"A float in an inner tube."

Gabby nodded. "Down a lazy stream."

"I can't be a lazy stream for you, Gabby. That's not what it's about between us."

"I know," she said softly. "You're the mid-Atlantic storm in my life. The only one I've ever had." She looked across at Graham. The cold, pale winter sky came through the doors behind her. "My one and only. To take out on lonely nights and remember."

"We don't have to settle for remembering. We don't have to walk away from this at all."

"I know that."

"I hear a *but* in your voice."

"In the end, I think we will."

"And if I promise we won't?"

"You can't make that promise. Any more than I can."

"I've fallen in love with you, Gabby," Graham said.

She nodded. "I know."

"That has to count for something."

"It does. I'm just not sure it will be enough."

"Come here," Graham said.

Gabby walked over to the bed where he sat and sank to her knees. Graham held her close while she cried. "I'm so scared, Graham. Because I've realized I never want to leave you," she said.

"Then don't leave me. We'll handle it somehow."

Gabby felt hot tears slide down her cheeks as she tried desperately to believe Graham's words.

Time and space rearranged themselves around her as she clung desperately to him and yearned for a world of tomorrows denied her by the same gods that made her who she was.

"Merry Christmas," Graham whispered. His body was over Gabby's, pinning her to the passion-rumpled sheets at exactly midnight.

"Merry Christmas." *My love, my life,* Gabby silently added.

She felt his body, his mouth crushing hers. Graham rolled over, pulling her with him. She rose up over him, his muscled body, and felt him take a deep breath and smile.

Yes, she thought as she lost herself in their two bodies and willed their life to never end.

The dark and timeless winds swept around the two lovers again and once again carried them to a place they'd never been before and would never find again.

Tennessee
December 30, 1993

The first time Theo made love to me when I came back
from the seminar, I kept waiting, wanting, needing,
and waiting. Then, when nothing happened, I realized
how much it had cost me. It was not only how wonderful
loving but being loved by Graham had been.

Gabby was certain Theo never knew she felt that way about making love after she'd been with Graham, never noticed the difference. She hadn't meant to let it affect her, hadn't realized she would. She still found it hard to believe so few nights and days with Graham spoiled that part of her life forever and made her spend years yearning to recapture what she had with him. She needed it, wished for it, prayed for it, all to no avail. The intensity of the storm was gone, and she floated on her old familiar stream again.

Now, Gabby was fifty-one years old, and it was too late to hope to feel that kind of passion again. Most nights, she worked late in the studio then crept into bed, silent and alone.

Even when Theo was home, she felt alone. It was no one's fault; it was simply the way things had happened and what she'd chosen for her life.

Gabby closed her eyes and returned once more to that vision.

Behind her lids, she sat in a dark bar with the man whose sketch she held so tenderly. Slowly, Gabby saw herself lift her face to Graham's for their first kiss.

In the solitary world of her studio, the tears fell again. The wind whipped around the house, so strong it felt like the house itself was breathing. The mimosa tree outside her window sent scratchy fingers across the glass.

Gabby got up, opened the miniblinds, and peered out. A layer of soft snow covered the ground, and flakes continued to swirl from the heavens. The scene was hauntingly familiar. Winters were always so hard. December and January sent her into tailspins of emotion. She and Theo lived in Florida almost ten years after leaving Boise, in southern Florida, where there were no winters. It was a little easier there, with no snow and with long, deserted stretches of beaches to walk along.

After Florida, they lived in Atlanta for a while before settling here in Tennessee. Theo traveled much less now. Gabby almost thought that made it harder. Plus it snowed here, so close to the mountains. The snow turned her heart as cold as it turned the world.

Gabby thought, not for the first time, if Graham wanted to reach her, he'd have no idea where to look. Her disappearance had been too complete. The temptation to drop an address and a phone number in the mail to him was sometimes almost impossible to resist. She wouldn't sign it. He'd know. At least she hoped he'd know.

After so much time, there was a worrisome doubt that maybe he wouldn't know, after all. That was the hardest thing, thinking that maybe he remembered her not at all.

Boise
Sunday, December 25, 1976

No holly, no mistletoe, no tree with shining lights, and
no presents, only love. The true reason for the season.
It was the most wonderful Christmas of my life.

"That was the best present you could give me," Graham whispered. The afterglow of the moment hung heavy around them.

He ran his hand down Gabby's flat stomach then moved back up to her neck and face.

"You're so beautiful," he breathed. "So wonderful, perfect, and sweet. I never knew anything could be so great in life."

"I'll never forget this Christmas, Graham," Gabby said. Her voice was soft and hushed. "Never." Her hand stroked his hard biceps, moved up over his powerful shoulder to his handsome face, loving and memorizing every last inch of him. Storing it away.

"Graham, I love you," she whispered. Once the dam had broken, the words had been spoken, Gabby couldn't seem to say them enough.

"I know. Amazing, isn't it?" Graham stroked her cheek. "Hungry?"

"For what?" Gabby asked; she was only half-teasing and heard Graham's quick intake of breath.

"Anything you want."

Gabby turned in the circle of his arms. She felt his heart pounding, heard his breath ragged in his chest.

"Oh yes," he whispered. "Just love me."

"Merry Christmas, my love." She smiled. "And I do love you, Graham."

"Snow's stopped." Graham was standing at the french doors when Gabby went out of the shower. He'd had room service take coffee and croissants to his room, then wheeled the cart into her room after the boy left.

"What's the weather report?" Gabby sat on the side of the bed and toweled her hair.

"Clearing. They hope to open the airport tonight." Graham had turned around when he heard her come into the room. Now he stood absolutely still and just watched her.

She smiled across at him. "Perfect." Their flight to Rum Springs left early in the morning. "Did you decide what we're doing about accommodations?"

Graham poured her coffee. "I called the inn and reserved a chalet instead of the room I had reserved."

"We're staying together?"

He nodded and took her coffee to her then stayed to rub her back. "It'll work. We simply don't answer the phone. We have the desk take messages. Whoever the message is for calls back."

Gabby took a sip of her coffee before she set it down on the bedside table. "Suppose the desk says something. Suppose the caller asks for the chalet, and the person on the desk asks which one of us they want to talk to. Suppose a call does get through, and the wrong person answers. Suppose someone gets hold of the records someday and finds both our names on the register for the same chalet at the same time."

"Suppose the world ends tomorrow," Graham countered. "Besides, I talked with the manager. They won't. They red-flag the registration, and that tells everybody to go into their caution mode. In other words, nobody knows nothing." He took the towel from Gabby and gently rubbed it down her hair.

"Everybody there knows. It marks us as having something to hide. One look and they'll guess it."

"Does that matter? If we get to be together?"

Gabby saw the plea in his eyes, and her heart gave in. "No," she said. "I guess it really doesn't."

"We'll have our own private place with a fireplace, a kitchen, the works. Even a hot tub."

"And everyone at the seminar will know we're staying together."

"I don't plan to spend much time at the seminar, do you?" Graham sat on the rumpled bed beside her and brushed a damp strand of the spun-gold hair off her face.

"Just enough to register and pick up a few schedules and things to prove I was there. Put in an occasional appearance," Gabby admitted.

"And we can do that separately, if you insist."

"We probably should," she said. "I doubt I'll know anyone there, but you might."

"I'm sure I will." Graham smiled.

"This is dangerous, isn't it?"

"Life is dangerous," he told her. "I'm willing to risk this. Are you?"

Gabby stared at him intently, her face open and vulnerable. When she spoke, it was with painful honesty and without pretense or reservation. She simply spoke her heart.

"For myself? Yes. You need to understand something, Graham. I'd give up my past, my present, and my future for just one more night with you. I'd destroy my life and my world for you," she said softly. "What I can't do is destroy anybody else's."

"I know that. We won't let it happen."

Gabby finally nodded. "All right."

The sudden ringing of the phone in his room startled them both.

"Patti," Gabby said. "Answer it, but close the door. I have to dry my hair."

By the time Graham got back, Gabby had her hair dried, her face lightly made up, and wore a pair of new wool slacks and her cashmere turtleneck. She was pulling on her riding boots.

"Going somewhere?"

"I have to go home and pack for tomorrow."

"I don't want to be away from you for even that long," Graham told her. "All I'll do is sit in this room and hold my breath until you get back."

"Then how do you feel about sliding down in the seat until I get the car safely in the garage?"

"I'd be honored, ma'am," he said.

Once more, Gabby went down ahead of him. In the parking lot, she started the car and left it to warm up while she brushed the snow and ice off the windows.

Five minutes later, Graham hurried across the windswept lot toward her.

"Get in before someone sees you," Gabby said. He'd stopped to watch her again.

Graham grinned as he opened the car door and slid inside. He was doing fine until she opened the trunk and dragged a snow shovel out then started digging out the mounds of snow the plow had buried the wheels under. That was too much, and Graham opened the car door and got out.

"I thought I told you to stay in the car," Gabby said.

"I will not sit in there and watch while you shovel this heavy stuff. You get in the car. This can't be the only navy Mercedes in Boise. Nobody will know it's not mine."

Graham's expression told Gabby arguing was useless. She opened her door, slid in, and then watched him shovel. Even through his leather jacket, she imagined she could see the ripple of his muscles. She could easily see his strong thighs working through his faded jeans. It made her feel all warm inside and made her heart beat faster.

He's wonderful, she thought, *and he doesn't even know it— totally natural, unrestrained, and sensual inside that beautiful body. Caring, so caring. I love him so desperately. I want to spend the rest of my life looking at him, touching him, and just loving him. Just being with him if that's all that can be. I just want to be near him for the rest of my days.* She was remembering that first morning when she awoke feeling someone was looking at her—she had turned her face slowly and found those piercing eyes looking at her and a beautiful smile on his face. She knew then that he had her heart for the rest of her days.

Tennessee
December 30, 1993

Was it Shakespeare who said 'time heals all wounds'?
Guess what? Whoever it was, they lied.

Gabby rubbed at the pain in her chest as she watched the snow fall past her studio window. The heaviness seemed worse tonight. Probably from the long walk in the intemperate weather. Either that or because of the doctor's grim warning that morning. *Tomorrow,* she promised herself. *Tomorrow, I'll have to talk to Theo. Tell him then get the damned surgery over with.*

Graham would be fifty-six now. Gabby thought about how vital and alive he'd been at thirty-nine when she'd met him and couldn't imagine him ever being any other way. Of course, she'd been thirty-four and figured she was immortal, just like her kids felt now. Gabby smiled, thinking of the kids again. What a life they'd given her. She couldn't imagine not having them. She hoped, at some point, Patti had given Graham a child. He'd wanted children so badly, and they were so important and wonderful and fulfilling as you got older.

She remembered holding BJ, her first grandchild. The ghosts of all her ancestors floated around her there in the corridor of the hospital. She saw her mother, her grandmother, her great-grandmother, all dead now, but all smiling down on them. Gabby fulfilled some rite of passage she never knew existed till then. Suddenly, and for all time, she understood what it meant to know a part of you would keep living after you were gone, generation after generation after generation.

It sobered Gabby, looking down into that tiny face, knowing

part of her was in this child she really had nothing to do with bringing into the world. It sobered her even more when she thought about how much she wished Graham could see him because thinking of Graham made Gabby realize she might never have held the tiny grandchild or even known anything about him.

They were that close to the brink in Rum Springs.

"I held her gently, afraid BJ would disappear in a cloud of smoke and be gone from me forever. Shattering my world and claiming my sanity."

"OK, you can get up now," Gabby said.

"I like it down here."

"That's only because you have your head in my lap."

Graham raised his head. "Is that a complaint?"

"Ah, no," Gabby said. "And you know it." She ran her fingers through his curls. "But the quicker we finish up here, the quicker we get back to the hotel and other things."

"Sold," Graham said. He sat up and looked around; they were in the garage, and the door was settling closed behind them. Gabby dropped the opener on the dashboard and swung out of the car. "Would you mind elaborating on those other things?"

"Not now, Graham." She laughed. "Later."

"OK." He shrugged. "Then why wasn't there any snow in your drive?"

"My god. Your mind flits around as bad as my kids do. We contract it out. Have it plowed."

"Smart. Which kid? The youngest, the oldest, or the two in between?"

"Take your pick," she said.

"I'd love to, Gabby," Graham said, all trace of banter gone. "Can I take all of them?"

"Don't, Graham, not here, please?"

She unlocked the door, swung it open, and waited for Graham to follow her inside. The door led into an airy large kitchen, all gleaming stainless steel and white ceramic tiles with a long butcher-block table running down the middle of the red glazed-brick floor. An antique rolltop desk sat in the corner between two huge bay windows filled with hanging plants. Copper pots were suspended from a rack over the stove.

"I can put on coffee, if you like," Gabby offered.

"I'll do it while you pack."

"Coffee's on the counter in a canister by the pot."

"Should I leave Theo a note?"

"Graham," Gabby warned.

She went down the hall to the bedroom, feeling very strange with Graham in the house. She hadn't thought it through. Taking Graham into the home she shared with Theo seemed like a slap in the face to that good man, more an act of treachery than sleeping with Graham somehow. She dragged her Gucci bag out of the closet and spread it open on the bed. She packed quickly with the ease of someone used to traveling—a few business outfits, slacks, jeans, sweaters, shoes, and boots. With her parka out of the front closet, the fur she bought on her last trip to New York, and what she had at the hotel, she'd be fine, she decided. She dragged the bag back to the kitchen. Graham was sitting at the table, watching the coffee perk. The face he turned up to her told Gabby his earlier banter had been covering a large dose of discomfort.

"I feel a little funny now that I'm here," he said quietly.

Gabby nodded. "I know. I was thinking the same thing."

"It makes Theo too real to me."

She nodded again. "Too personal. Like reading someone else's mail."

"Exactly." Graham shrugged. "I just wanted surroundings to place you in."

When it's over, she added silently. *Don't think like that. Don't spoil what you've been given.* "Then let's take a quick tour and get the hell out of here."

"I don't think so," Graham said. He got up and turned the coffee off. "I think I prefer to remember you in places we shared. Places that were ours, not a place you share with someone else."

Thirty minutes later, they were back at the hotel. Gabby's phone was ringing when she opened the door. As usual, Graham would wait five minutes before following. Gabby grabbed the phone and fell across the bed.

"Hello?"

"Hey, miss us?"

"Theo. You know I do."

"I tried to call earlier. The desk clerk said he thought he saw you go out." Gabby's heart pounded. Thank God she and Graham went out separately.

"Had to sneak home and pack."

"That's right. What made Jack decide you needed to go to a seminar, anyway?"

"You know Jack. It could've been anything from bad pâté to good scotch."

Theo laughed. "Too true."

"How's Christmas in Minnesota?"

"I know why we visit so seldom," Theo said solemnly. "The noise level and confusion are unnerving."

Gabby laughed just as Graham pushed the connecting door open. "You leaving in the morning?" she asked Theo.

"Actually, I'm booked out tonight. I couldn't take any more of a good thing."

Graham went over and sat down on the bed beside Gabby. She was stretched out on her stomach, her head toward the wall. He kissed her slack-clad rear end.

"Don't blame you. How are the kids?"

"Be prepared to completely retrain them when they come home."

"Don't we always?"

"I think this may be the worst ever. Your brother's here too."

"Oh lord." Gabby's only brother was twenty-three, and the kids worshipped him. It was decidedly mutual.

"Do you have a number where you'll be next week?" Theo asked.

"I'll call and give it to you when I get there."

"OK," Theo said. "I'm at the usual. I didn't even give up my room. Just left everything there until I got back. Except for what I needed here."

"That was easier, I'm sure. When are you coming home?"

"On the red-eye, Friday morning around eight. I'll have breakfast and wait for you at the airport since you're coming in at ten."

"Sounds good." It didn't. Gabby didn't want him there. She wanted to say good-bye to Graham before she had to say hello to Theo, wanted every last minute she could get.

"I miss you," Theo said.

"Me too. Kiss the kids?"

"Gabby, they have so many presents, they won't even notice. Trust me."

"Probably haven't even noticed I'm not there."

"I think one of them mentioned it in passing. Just before your mother decided they could start opening presents."

"She's really enjoying this, isn't she?"

"Your mother thinks she's in heaven, of course, so is your dad. I hate to say it, but I don't think anybody's missed you. Except me."

"Tell them all 'Merry, merry' for me."

"Will do." There was a pause. "Don't stay cooped up in that room all day, OK? It's Christmas. Go down for dinner, have a couple of drinks in the bar. See if you can't find another stranded soul to talk to for a while."

"I'll see what I can do, Theo," Gabby promised softly.

Later, much later, she and Graham did go down for dinner. They didn't even go down separately. They were stranded at the hotel, prisoners of the weather. They decided they could always claim they met in the elevator.

"I can't wait," Graham said. He sat across the candlelit table from her, twirling his after-dinner brandy.

"For what?" Gabby had her shoe off and was running her foot up his pant leg. She was smiling as she teased him with her toes.

"Having you alone in Rum Springs."

"I know. How many people do you think you'll know?"

"I was thinking about that. I don't think I'm going to let it bother me," Graham said.

"What do you mean?"

"It's the seventies," he said. "I don't think anybody will say anything. Even if they figure it out. Would you? In their place?"

"Of course not. I'd think it wasn't any of my business."

"Exactly. Besides," he said slowly. "It won't really make any difference if we decide to continue this past next week, now, will it?"

Gabby looked away. "Don't push. Please. I'm dealing with this the best I can."

Silence answered her. When she turned back, Graham was watching her with pleading eyes.

"Please," she whispered.

"Okay," he finally said. "Then, for your sake, we'll treat this as a hypothetical discussion. Say we are going to walk away from this wonderful gift we've been given. Even then, I'm still very torn, you know? I desperately want to show you off to the people I know will be there. Stand up and shout, 'Hey, see this beautiful, wonderful, awesome lady? Well, she's with me.' Something like that, anyway." He gave her his most appealing and boyish shrug.

Gabby gave him a horrified look.

"But I want to protect you too," he added quickly.

"Sometimes you scare me," she said. "I'm afraid you may actually do something like that."

He shrugged again then gave her his intoxicating smile.

"Listen, cowboy, I think we better stick to the protection idea.

If someone does see us together, we're both at the same seminar. We can pretend we met up casually, decided to grab a bite to eat or whatever."

"I don't do *whatever* casually."

Graham's voice was deadly serious again and haunted Gabby's senses. His hand was under the table, casually stroking the bottom of her foot, running up her leg as far as he could reach.

"I know you have proved your *whatever* is anything but casual," Gabby said solemnly.

"Keep it up," Graham warned, "and you'll go upstairs without dessert."

Gabby gave him her wickedest grin. "And if I volunteer to be dessert?"

Graham drew in his breath sharply. "You go ahead. I'll pay the bill."

Gabby laughed and got up while Graham tried desperately to catch their waiter's eye. He caught up with her at the elevator.

"That was quick," she said.

"I told the waiter you were waiting upstairs to be my dessert. He hurried, and not only that, he did it all with a smile on his face."

"You did not." Gabby reached over and pressed the up button again.

"Are you sure about that?"

Gabby looked up at him. In the dim lighting by the elevator, his eyes were almost emerald and his hair had a dark golden-red sheen to it. He'd dressed for dinner in a dark pinstripe suit. She thought he was the most incredibly handsome man she'd ever seen. Gabby longed to reach over and touch him, just touch him.

She needed to reassure herself he was real, reassure herself she wasn't dreaming all this.

"I'm not sure about very much right now," she said. "Except what I plan to do once we're upstairs."

"What's taking this stupid elevator so long?" Graham asked. "Has the mule gone home for the night?"

"I feel downright wicked," Gabby whispered into the curve where Graham's neck and shoulder met. She breathed deeply, loving the scent of his skin.

"Why is that?" He smiled and brushed loving fingers through her hair.

"Do you realize, since I met you, I've spent much more of my time undressed than dressed."

"It's hard to do what we spend most of our time doing if we're going to be dressed," Graham said seriously.

"Oh, my word, you're awful."

"You didn't think that a few minutes ago."

Gabby gave his arm a playful jab. Loving this man was fun. "I can't believe I'm actually flying to Rum Springs with you tomorrow."

"Why can't you believe it?"

"Is this the way you expected to spend Christmas?"

"Not hardly."

"Or next week?"

"No," Graham said slowly. "I feel like the gods took pity on me and sent me an angel for Christmas. Then decided to let me keep her an extra week."

Gabby laughed. "It wasn't the angel, Graham. It was the devil."

"What are you talking about?"

Briefly, she explained about her little devil and angel conscience figures. "And it was definitely not the angel who sent me into your arms," she finished.

"You're not only beautiful and smart and sexy," Graham said, laughing with her. "You're also crazy."

"Crazy about you," she said.

"I hate to sound like a broken record, but it doesn't have to end next week, you know." Graham turned on his side and looked at Gabby earnestly, his hand resting on her hip. "You travel, I travel. We could make opportunities. Even if you won't talk about divorce, we can keep that option open."

"Can we? Graham, I'm not so sure."

"Why not?"

Gabby pulled away and sat on the side of the bed. "I looked up and saw you on that podium. I felt the fire between us and knew we were going to be together, Graham. Never mind that I preach free will and choices to my children. I really didn't have all of this in my mind. I wanted you, and I saw a way to get you. It happened. Period." She shook her head. "But I'm not sure I could set out to deliberately cheat on Theo. If I packed my bags, left my house, caught a plane, knowing I was going to meet you. Well..." She shrugged.

"Because you still love him?"

"I've been married to him for fourteen, almost fifteen, years. I've given birth to four children he fathered. The kind of love Theo and I have grows on you. Becomes a habit. That's its strength. I told you, Graham. He's a good man. A good husband and a good father." She smiled sadly at Graham. "And you still love Patti too."

Graham nodded. "Yes. But not like this."

"Nothing else like this exists," Gabby said. "It never has before, and it never will again. I don't even think something this intense would be strong enough to be sustained over the distance."

"I'm willing to find out."

"What if part of its attraction is that it's self-limiting? Have you thought about that? What if we tear up two marriages then decide we made a mistake?"

"This is not a mistake. This is the most on-purpose thing I've ever done."

"But don't you see?" Gabby gently stroked his cheek. "We're trying to pack a whole lifetime of loving in the short time given us. Maybe that's why it's so special."

"This, Gabby, would always be special. No matter what the

circumstances," Graham said. "Do you know what I felt when I looked down in that audience and saw you?"

"No." Gabby turned back to him, nude and ethereal in the pale light from the lamps. Graham gently stroked one slim thigh.

"Promise not to laugh?"

"I promise," she said.

"I felt connected to you on some primitive plane beyond all reason. I felt time rearrange itself around me and make room for you in my life."

Gabby laughed.

"You promised not to laugh," he said.

"I'm not laughing at you. I'm laughing with you."

"That's what they all say."

"I am," Gabby said. "Really. Because I imagined I could see and smell man's first fire burning."

"You did?"

Gabby grinned. "Yeah. But then I decided it was the mushrooms I had for dinner."

"I didn't have any mushrooms," Graham said. "Smarts. So why was I included in your hallucination?"

Gabby shrugged. "Just lucky?"

"Do you want me to finish this or not? Here I am, trying to bare my soul to you, and all you do is make fun."

Gabby's eyes were twinkling. She really was laughing with him. She really had felt the things he was describing. "I'm sorry. Please, go ahead."

"OK," he said. "Be still and listen. We were alone in the world except for these ancient mastodons that roamed around us just out of sight."

"Mastodons, huh?"

"I told you to be quiet and listen. Mastodons, you know, those ancient elephant things."

"I know what they are, Graham." She was trying so hard to control her smile. She was almost successful.

Graham gave her an exasperated look. "There's only one way

to shut you up," he declared. He leaned across and kissed her long and hard. As the kiss grew and blossomed, he raised himself over her and gently settled his weight on her slender body, pinning her to the bed beneath him. He was suddenly breathless and needy. His lips moved down to her, caressing her and loving her.

Gabby moaned softly, all trace of her earlier banter gone.

"And you were the only man in the world at that moment," she whispered. "And I fell hopelessly, insanely in love with you, Graham Wright."

"And my life began in that instant," Graham said. "We can't give that up—I can't ever give you up, Gabby."

"Do we have a choice?" Gabby replied.

Tennessee
December 30, 1993

It was like the dates and times were written on an ancient scroll and covered by the glaciers. Rested upon by the bones of dinosaurs and washed in the floods. Both for the beginning and the end.

They hadn't had a choice. Not really, not in the end, and not being who they were. Honesty and decency sent both Gabby and Graham home bearing a secret and a sense of loss almost too heavy to endure. It sent them both back with the knowledge that there was a black hole in the universe. It had swallowed them up for a brief moment in time and space and taught them what love was.

Gabby sighed deeply and touched his sketch again. *Graham, Graham,* she thought. *I would love to see your face, just one more time before I die.* Her thoughts shocked Gabby. "Geez, you're morbid tonight," she whispered to herself. "Are you that worried about the surgery?"

She heard a bump in the hall then padding footsteps on the stairs. Annie was going to bed. Gabby would find her later in the middle of the king-size bed, snuggled against Theo. It was where she'd slept every night since he took her home. They never even allowed the children to get away with that.

Gabby closed her eyes and leaned back again. Suddenly, the ringing of the phone split the quiet night. She lurched up and grabbed the one on her desk, her pulse racing like a phone in the night always made it do.

"Hello?"

"Mom?" It was Samantha's voice. "Are you all right?"

"I'm fine, Sam. Why?" *Ah, no, Sam. My heart is breaking. My memories are haunting me. My soul cries out to see a smiling, golden-haired, green-eyed face again. Just once, even from a great distance.*

"I'm not sure," her youngest daughter sighed. "I just got worried about you. I was on my way home from work, and this little voice said, 'Call Mom.'"

"Just in my studio, working late," Gabby said.

There was the slightest pause then Sam's soft voice. "It's that time again, isn't it?"

"What time? What are you talking about, Sam?"

"I'm not sure. All I know is every year about this time, you get all sad and lonely. You've done it for as long as I can remember. You tried to hide it from all of us, but I always knew."

"I just hate the holidays, Sam, that's all." Gabby tried to put reassurance in her voice.

"No, that's not all. Mom, I'm not a kid anymore. Why don't you talk to me? It might help."

Sam was the one Gabby would tell if she told anyone. Sam was the one she always felt the closest to. Probably because her youngest daughter stayed home the longest, only moving out on her own when Gabby and Theo left Atlanta.

"Sam, it's not something I can ever talk about." Gabby's voice was suddenly empty across the wires. She knew it but couldn't help it. "I can tell you you're right. There's something about this date. Something that makes me feel like I've earned the right and paid the dues to be sad this one night of the year. We have to let it go at that. I'm sorry."

"Can't I help?"

"Nobody can, darling. Besides, it's something that happened a lifetime ago. Happened in a different world and to a different person."

"I hate him," Sam said quietly.

Gabby's pulse jumped. "You hate who?"

"Whoever he is, to make you so sad."

Gabby felt the tears start down her cheeks again. "You're wrong, Sam. It was a decision I made." She took a deep breath and wiped at her tears. "This is my one night of indulgence, Sam. Can't we just leave me to it? By morning, I'll be fine."

"Will you call me?"

"Of course."

There was a pause, while Gabby listened to the whistle of the storm-rattled long-distance lines. "Mom? I love you."

"And I love you, Sam," Gabby whispered. "More than you'll ever know." *More than any of you will ever know.*

Rum Springs
Monday, December 26, 1976

Everything and nothing went before this time.
Everything and nothing will follow.

"Graham, I am so excited," Gabby whispered. She leaned over and looked out the window of the little silver Otter as it soared over the mountains.

"I can tell." Graham smiled at her.

Gabby knew she'd made getting this far a real hassle. She made Graham take a limo to the airport while she drove, then insisted they go through an elaborate pretense of accidentally running into each other at the gate. Once in the air, with a chance to look over the other passengers and realize she didn't know any of them, Gabby had finally relaxed.

The sky outside the window of the little plane was a brilliant winter blue. White clouds raced along beside it in a playful game of tag. The drone of the motors made conversation almost impossible. It also had a soothing, almost hypnotic, effect on the passengers. Gabby watched the morning slip past the window, holding on to Graham's hand like it was a lifeline to her happiness. It was. In time, she felt his hand relax and looked over at him. He was asleep.

As Gabby was watching him, her heart lurched in her chest and she felt tears forming behind her lids again. *God, I love this man. How can I leave him? How can I even consider it? What would my life be like without him? How can I settle for what used to be when I know what can be?* She swiped at her tears with her free hand. *And if I don't leave Graham, if I go with my heart, what will I tell Theo? How can I make Theo's world all right if I leave him for Graham?*

Gabby looked back out the windows. The plane was beginning its descent. *God*, she prayed. *Don't ask me to make this decision. Please. I can't. I don't know how.* The change in altitude, the change in pressure, the change in the sound of the motors, all conspired to stop Gabby's silent pleas by waking Graham.

"Sorry," he said, rubbing the sleep away from his eyes. "I didn't mean to go to sleep on you."

"You need your rest," Gabby said, hoping he didn't see the sheen of tears in her eyes. "After all, you are older than I am."

"Five years," Graham said. "Hardly any time at all." *Unless I can't spend it with you*, Gabby thought. *Then every day will be forever.* "You're an old man," she teased. He leaned over and kissed the tip of her nose. "Wait till we get to our chalet," he said. "I'll show you old man."

"Promises, promises," Gabby said.

"You want me to show you now?" Graham let his hand fall down to her knee. "Get in the bathroom."

Gabby blushed furiously. "Stop that," she said. "We're on an airplane, for God's sake."

"You never heard of the mile-high club?"

"Of course I have. But I have no intention of joining it."

"Then shape up with this old-man stuff. I'm big enough to pick you up and carry you to the bathroom."

"Why don't you just hit me over the head with your club then drag me by the hair?"

Graham pretended to consider her suggestion. "Works for me," he finally said. Luckily, the "fasten your seat belts" sign came on at that exact moment.

"Saved by the bell," Graham told her.

The little plane almost brushed the tops of the tall trees as they landed in the small airport between the majestic mountain peaks. The airport was an A-frame chalet with plumes of smoke coming out of its broad chimney. Graham collected their luggage, and they followed the rest of the passengers to a horse-drawn trolley. Gabby had never seen so many skis and poles in one place. It was obvious most of those deplaning went to play, not spend time doing anything as plebeian as attending a seminar.

Once all the luggage and people were shuffled aboard the trolley, its wizened driver gave a "Giddyap," and the horses left the airport behind and wound their way through the picturesque little town.

Wooden sidewalks lined snow-packed streets; traffic lights were nonexistent, as was anything but foot traffic and the horse-drawn trolleys. Small, exclusive shops fronted the sidewalks, interspersed with period saloons and restaurants. The street signs were wooden, with names like Alpine Way and Ski Hill burned into them. The signs on the shops were discreet brass plates. Even the Christmas lights lining the streets were all white; the wreaths on the poles, silver.

They left the town proper and traveled down a snow-tamped road beside forests green and primeval. Resorts masquerading as small Swiss villages were set into the hillside between breaks in the trees.

An air of celebration and good humor hung in the air, and the surrounding mountain slopes were a riot of bright colors as skiers raced down them at breakneck speeds.

A half mile out of town, the driver stopped at Graham and Gabby's destination. Close to the street, a huge chalet right out of Heidi's Alps stood in the sunshine, bearing a sign that read "Rum Springs Inn." Behind it, a large four-story building carried out the chalet's design. To the right, disappearing into the pine growth on the mountain, two dozen small chalets basked in the mountain light. It was one of these Graham had reserved.

Graham got their luggage again, and they started up the walk through the snowy quiet. In the lobby, a fire crackled and soared in the great stone fireplace. Leather couches, love seats, and chairs, all in saddle tan, gathered in conversation pits around the fire. Sunlight streamed through mullioned windows two stories tall. A stuffed black bear, fully seven feet tall, stood just inside the entrance in a fearsome pose.

"Relative of yours?" Gabby asked, nodding to the bear.

"Uncle Slim," Graham said, not missing a beat. "Want to meet him?"

"I think not," Gabby said. "He's even older than you."

"You are on dangerous ground," Graham warned her.

They passed a sign propped up on a wooden easel that said "Ethics Roundtable Registration." An arrow pointed to a room off the lobby to their left. Its doors were closed, and a handmade sign on them read, "You're early. Registration starts at four." As they neared the desk, Gabby's nervousness returned. When she found out they were both required to sign the register, it hit a ten on the Richter scale.

She managed to say, as the lights wavered around her, the conversations were burning her ears, "Please don't give out any information to anyone who calls." She was choking on the smell of old cigarettes. Ghosts followed her with the faces of her children and Theo as she finished registering then said, "I'll see you all tomorrow."

Graham gave her a worried look. "Not a bad idea, think I'll crash in a minute too." He stayed at the table with the others and let her leave alone.

When Graham left and passed the receptionist, he paused a moment and said, "What the lady tried to tell you means"—as he slid his card back across the desk—"is we're not here together. Thank you for your help."

The clerk, a muscular young man out of a commercial for Royal Scandinavian Airlines, smiled at the two of them. "I understand, sir. No problem." He smiled as he stuck a red tab on the corner of the registration slip as promised.

"And don't ring the room. Take messages. Do people ask for guests by chalet numbers or by name?"

"By name only, we don't give out room numbers or the names

of guests. We've done a lot of this," he assured him. "There's nothing to worry about."

Graham relayed the reassuring message to Gabby, who was waiting outside.

"I hope not," Gabby muttered.

Outside again, Graham grinned down at her. "It's that direction. Do you want me to wait and walk three paces behind you? Or can we do this together?"

"Together," Gabby said. "We'll just pretend you're the bellhop."

"Yas'm, Ms. Scarlett."

"Shut up, Graham, and look like the hired help." She grinned.

They moved up the path to one of the small chalets set in the pines against the rising mountains. It was another A-frame, and it was surrounded by wooden decks and nestled among the firs. A massive stone chimney covered one outside wall. There wasn't another soul out on the walkways as they went up the steps, and Gabby breathed a sigh of relief when Graham got the key in the lock and pushed the door open.

"Can I carry you over the threshold?" he whispered against her ear.

"Get inside before somebody sees us, will you please?"

Graham laughed and pushed the door open. Inside, a small kitchen was to the left of the entry. The living room was down two steps. A huge stone fireplace completely filled one living room wall. The sliding doors to the back deck looked out over pristine, unmarked snow and stands of dark-green firs liberally frosted with white. On the stone floor, right inside the back doors, a hot tub burbled happily. A steep winding staircase led up to a loft bedroom. The bed, with plump pillows and a deep down comforter, was visible from below.

"Oh god, it's perfect," Gabby said.

"Our hideaway," Graham said. He took the bags to the stairs, set them down, then went back and took her in his arms. "I wanted this to be something perfect in our imperfect world," he whispered. "Something to remember."

Gabby took a deep breath. "It will be," she assured him softly. She drank in every detail of the little chalet, using an artist's eye to capture it, the light coming through the back windows and slanting across the massive stone hearth. The dust motes floating in the shaft of sunshine, the warm, rich paneling on the walls, the scent of pine from the logs laid in the fireplace, the gloss of the pegged wooden floors. She knew she would replay every small thing in her memory for the rest of her life. Whatever happened.

"I'll take the bags up."

Gabby nodded and turned her head away, not wanting Graham to see the sudden tears that had welled up in her eyes with her last thought. *Please, God*, she prayed. *Let me find some way to keep what we have found together. Please, oh please, Lord, don't ever take him from me. Just find a way to take me from him. I can't stand the pain I am going through in just the thought of living without him. Please, God, don't ever take him from me.* And the tears fell from her face.

Since Gabby needed something to do to stop her thoughts in the downward tumble they seemed determined to take and the fire was already laid, she went over to the mantle, took down long fireplace matches, and kneeled to light the waiting logs. The dry cured wood caught immediately.

"Were you a Girl Scout?" Graham asked. Errand upstairs finished, he went up behind Gabby and wrapped his arms around her again.

"Not even close—in my spare time I hung around Daddy's brokerage firm after school." Gabby leaned back against his strong body. Safe again. "We need to go to the grocery. Pick up coffee and some stuff for meals."

Graham turned her around. "Did I hear you say *we?*"

"Yes," Gabby said. "I've decided this is our time, Graham. Whatever the future holds or doesn't hold, we have this. We have now. And I won't let anything destroy it. I can't." Gabby looked up at Graham. He was looking back at her with the eyes that burned memories on her soul. "I won't let the life we left behind interfere with our time together up here."

"Can you separate the two?" he asked. "I'm not sure I can."

"I have to. I'm not Theo's wife up here. I'm not the mother of four children. I'm Gabby Franks, and I'm here with the man I love more than I love life. This is my world for the next few days."

"Gabby, if you let this slip away from us, you know, this world is all you'll have to take out and relive on cold winter nights."

"And sunny summer days. And anytime it's three o'clock in the morning in my soul. I know, Graham, I know."

"And if we let this go, there are going to be a lot of those."

Gabby nodded. "Yes, I know for this time I will hold such moments in my memory and lock them there tightly."

Graham tightened his arms around her and kissed her deeply. A rainbow of colors went off behind Gabby's eyes. Her mind worked feverishly to store every small thing away—the gentleness of Graham's touch and the hard strength of his body against hers, the masculine smell of him. The way her heart strained upward in her chest, hoping to blend with his forever, the jumbled emotions of love and fulfillment and need that coursed through her body, the feelings of discovery and happiness he brought to her world. The warmth of the fire against her back was almost as warm as Graham's touch. These things burned themselves across Gabby's memory. She needed them all. Needed them desperately for now, for later, quite possibly for forever. At least to the end of her time.

Later, after they made love on the white fur rug in front of the crackling fire, Graham lay with his arms around her, her head nestled against his chest.

Gabby wished the world would end right now. While Graham still held her.

The light outside changed. Afternoon sun crept into the chalet filtered by the massive trees.

"We need to check for messages."

"And get registered for the seminar," Graham added.

"And at least go buy some coffee for morning."

"I don't want to let you go long enough to do any of that," Graham whispered against her ear.

"Then we won't." Gabby rolled over on top of him and moved her hands deliberately down his body.

Graham drew in a shaky breath and buried his hands in her hair. Groceries, the seminar, as well as the world would have to wait.

Hours later, Graham watched her dress. "Make me a grocery list, and I'll run to the store while you finish getting ready to register."

"No."

"No?"

Gabby was standing by the bed, suitcase open, wearing nothing but her silk undies. Her body was a real vision as always. *As always*, he echoed to himself.

"I want to do everything together." She looked up at Graham, her eyes luminous in the afternoon light. "Please?"

"Anything you want." *Baby, anything.*

"This is the most special thing I've ever done. I need to store all of it up, Graham. Hide it away in the corners of my mind."

"I'll wait."

"Thank you." Gabby grabbed a pair of black stretch ski pants and pulled them on. They molded her firm bottom and slender hips like a second skin. She added a black silk turtleneck that emphasized her full breasts. Her shape was clearly visible against the tight fabric.

"You're so unbelievably beautiful," Graham breathed.

Gabby looked across at him as she tucked the shirt into the tight waistband of the ski pants. "I love you," she whispered.

Graham nodded. "I know that." He tugged a heavy ski sweater

over his head while she sat on the bed and laced up a pair of her soft black après-ski boots.

She started to braid her long hair.

"No," he said softly. "Leave it down."

Gabby's eyes locked with his, and her breath caught at the love and longing reflected in them.

"All right." She went to the dresser, ran a brush through her hair, and shook it out. It was like a cloud settling over her shoulders.

"Thank you."

They stood across the bedroom from each other, hearts full, eyes searching, memorizing love.

Finally, Gabby broke the spell by grabbing her ski parka. It was a pure winter white, fitted, cinched in at her waist. Her leather gloves matched it perfectly. "Ready?"

"Never," Graham said.

Gabby knew exactly what he meant.

The afternoon was cold and crisp and had a hint of snow in the air as they locked the door to the chalet and started down the walkway. Gabby linked her arm through Graham's and rested her head against his shoulder.

"Somebody might see you," Graham teased softly.

"I don't care. I told you. This is my time. I won't waste it." There was a break in her normally strong voice. "I can't."

"Good."

They walked the short distance into town, arm in arm, lost in each other. They went down the wooden sidewalks to the small grocery, bought coffee, french bread, cheese, fresh fruit, cocoa, plus a few staples. It was food for lovers, easy and undemanding.

They stopped at the liquor store, where they bought Jack Daniel's for him, margarita mix and tequila for her.

The snow scrunched under their feet as Gabby and Graham made their way back to the chalet. A few flakes of soft powder began to fall. It melted on their hair, dusted their eyelashes white, and turned their cheeks rosy.

The quiet was absolute as they wound the short distance through the deserted woods. Revelers weren't out yet. Skiers were still schussing down slopes. For a moment, the two lovers could imagine they were alone in the world.

As they went out on the walkway, Graham's quiet voice broke her reverie. "Intruder off the starboard bow," he said.

"What?" Gabby turned uncomprehending eyes up to him.

"An acquaintance. Coming our way. There." Graham nodded.

A gray-haired man trudged along the snowy walk. His collar was turned up, and he looked like he was freezing. He went straight toward Graham and Gabby.

"Graham," the man said, their paths meeting. "Heard you'd be here." He looked at Gabby with appraising eyes.

"Hank." Graham nodded. "I'd shake, but my hands seem to be full."

"So I see. Staying in one of the chalets?" His glance and question included Gabby.

"He's being a gentleman and helping me back from town. It seems I bought more than I could handle." Gabby stepped in smoothly. "Gabriella Franks," she introduced herself.

"Franks? Franks? Gabriella Franks?" Hank frowned in concentration before enlightenment finally registered across his face. "Of course, you are vice president at Lord and Young's. You're Jack Young's golden girl."

"So they tell me," Gabby said. "And you are?"

"Impressed." Hank's eyes swept her body.

"Hank Clifton," Graham filled in. "Clifton and Webb, attorneys-at-law. Corporate law, Dirty old man in his spare time."

"I've done some local work for your boss," Hank explained to Gabby, ignoring Graham's remark. "Helped him with some property acquisitions and the frightening web of California restrictions."

"Glad to meet you," she said. "I assume I'll see you later at registration?"

"Of course," Hank said. "Why don't you see if you can lose old Graham here. I'll buy you a drink?"

Gabby laughed. "Thank you, but I'm afraid Jack didn't send me up here to socialize. Dr. Wright was just kind enough to help me out."

"Well, next time you need help"—Hank winked at Gabby—"I'm in 211."

"I'll keep that in mind. Later." Gabby swept away regally, leaving Graham to say his good-byes and follow her.

"I'm impressed," Graham said when he caught up with her.

"What? Handling ol' Hank? Comes with the territory. And I didn't even ask what in the world a lawyer was doing at an ethics conference. Aren't you proud of me?"

"More than you'll ever know," Graham said softly. "Even if you give me the rest of my lifetime to tell you."

"I'm trying," Gabby said. "Trying to figure out some way..."

"I know. Me too."

They walked the rest of the way to their chalet in silence. At the door, Graham said, "I thought we weren't going to hide this week."

"Not hiding, Graham," Gabby said. "But not flaunting it either. Not rubbing Hank's face in it. He'll figure it out soon enough, if he hasn't already. What I said gives him an out. He can acknowledge it or not. According to his own code of ethics." She waited while Graham unlocked the door and pushed it open. "There's a certain social conduct—it's wise to stay inside," Gabby finished.

"Why?" Graham asked. He took the bags she was carrying and put them on the kitchen counter with the ones he'd taken in.

"So you don't give them any reason to dislike you or be jealous of you. Those two things are very bad for business."

"Must be why you're in business and I'm not."

"Must be." Gabby smiled. "I worry about profit-and-loss statements. You worry about publishing your books, teaching your classes, scheduling your next lecture." She shrugged. "Same difference. We're both dependent on something to keep us where we are. Or propel us further up the ladder."

"And you're very good at this, aren't you?"

"I know what I'm doing. I play their game well. Why?"

Graham shrugged. "New side of you, that's all."

"And you prefer the soft side?"

Tennessee
Thursday, December 30, 1993

*Empty days, sleepless nights, check marks against the calendar of time.
Year after year, each filled with more agony than the last.*

"So much," Gabby whispered. Tonight was the worst anniversary she could remember, probably because of that damned book. The pain and loss were deeper and more compelling than in any time in the past. "Why can't it get easier?" she asked softly. "Why can't I forget you, Graham? Why do you still have this hold over my life?"

Because you still love him, her heart whispered. *You only gave him up in theory, never in reality. Because you really believed someday you'd be in his arms again. Tonight, you've quit believing that. Tonight, reality is winning.*

The thought jolted Gabby hit her like a moment of truth. She sat there, stunned. She had believed that. When her duties were done, when she satisfied her responsibilities, when Graham satisfied his, they'd brush the years away and come together again. On that day, they'd reclaim what they gave up so long ago. It was just a matter of time and patience and believing.

"Dear God," she whispered. "Have I waited all these years for something that can never be? The years will run out before our responsibilities do."

My mind, my honor, my sense of right and wrong, those things sent me home to Theo and the kids. My heart never agreed. It waited patiently for its time to come, a fluttering bird with silky wings trapped painfully inside my chest. And now I have to tell it that it must now stay trapped there forever? I have to put the dream to rest. There is no fairy-tale world, then, now, or ever.

The quiet gathered around Gabby, the darkness pressed against the windows, begging to go into her safe and secure world. The wind whispered to her. *Unless. Unless. Unless Graham is still at USC...*

Rum Springs
Wednesday, December 28, 1976

I waited for her, not even knowing I was waiting.
I waited through years of ordinary life for this one and only
time when my spirit would soar above the clouds where man
was never intended to be yet only the soaring eagles could go.

During the brief night, seven inches of fresh powder fell. Gabby stood on the back deck in the circle of Graham's arms, safe from the world. A dazzling surface of purest white stretched as far as they could see.

"I feel very insignificant," Gabby said, "against this awesome backdrop." Silently she thought, *And I realize our problems don't count for much in the big scheme of things. It's no wonder God doesn't listen to our pleas.*

She felt the stillness, listened to the infinite silence, and was absorbed by the solitude.

"I bet the world looked like this when it was first created," Graham said in a whisper. "I wish we'd been there then. No world, just us, alone and together."

They'd talked far into the night but solved nothing.

Graham didn't want to lose Gabby. Gabby didn't want to lose Graham.

Amid the tears, they couldn't find a choice that wouldn't tear the children's or spouses' worlds apart. The darkness around the bed provoked fear and uneasiness in Gabby before she finally fell asleep.

She woke at first light with Graham's strong arms wrapped around her tightly. *Like they should be,* she thought. *Around me—that's where they belong.* The painful tension had receded over the night, and Gabby vowed to keep it away from them today, somehow keep the pain at bay.

When the coffee started to wend its fragrance through the chalet and out to the deck, Gabby and Graham went inside. "Your turn to pick up messages," she told him as she filled his cup.

"Must I? Couldn't we ignore them, just one day?"

"Theo's in New York on business," Gabby said. "Consumed by his own world. Sure of me, where I am, and what I'm doing. He'll merely assume we missed each other." She looked at Graham steadily. "Are you as sure of Patti?"

"What do you mean?"

"Will she detour past here to see you when she leaves her parents? If she doesn't hear from you, will she leave early to spend time up here with you?"

It took Graham only a minute to see Gabby's point. "I'll go get the messages." He sighed.

Gabby's smile was sad as she spoke. "You see, Graham, you don't want to hurt Patti any more than I want to hurt Theo."

"No, I don't," he admitted. "If I wanted to hurt her, I'd hope she would come up here. Find us together. End the charade." He blew out his breath. "There's not a third choice in all this, I suppose?"

"If there is, I can't find it."

"And you've tried."

"Yes," Gabby whispered. "From the moment I laid eyes on you."

Graham nodded sadly. "Yeah. Me too."

"Come on," Gabby said. "Finish your coffee. I'll buy you breakfast at the Chateau."

"And we'll both pick up the messages?" Graham asked.

"Chicken," Gabby teased gently.

They stayed for the morning meetings. It was a chance to pick up information and documents to take home with them.

It seemed a wise sacrifice to make. When they broke for lunch, Gabby insisted they walk into town again. "I want to pick up something for the kids," she told Graham. "They're souvenir freaks. Plus, I always bring them something when I'm away."

"I want to take you back to the chalet," Graham said. "I want to make love to you all afternoon."

"Later," Gabby promised. The hand she laid on his cheek was as tender as the touch of spring rain.

"Shop fast," Graham said.

The look Gabby saw in his eyes made her weak and shaky. Would she ever again see that look on any man's face? Or would a man ever again see that look on her face?

In the shelter of the pines on the way to town, Graham pulled her to him and bent to kiss her upturned face. His hands slid inside her parka and held her.

"Sure you want to go on into town?" he asked.

"I'm sure I don't." Gabby felt breathless and needy. "But I'm going anyway."

"Oh well, I tried."

"I know you did, Graham, we'll hurry."

At one of the small shops, Gabby bought four sweatshirts with the Rum Springs logo across them, one for each child, and three silver ski charms for the girls' bracelets. She got Jay a ski patch for his parka.

"Get Patti something," she told Graham as she paid for her purchases.

"You're not getting Theo anything."

"Theo's not female. Patti is."

"What's that mean?"

"Theo would think I'd gone crazy. Patti will think you miss her."

"I don't."

Gabby glanced up at him while the girl behind the counter arranged her gifts in a shopping bag. "It would be better if you let her think you do."

"Then you buy her something."

Graham walked outside and leaned back against the wall of the store. Gabby watched him with sad eyes. She could feel his pain, the pain she vowed to keep away from them today, through the brick walls of the pricey little shop.

She went back to the jewelry case and selected a thin gold chain with a pair of crossed skis hanging from it. It was delicate and expensive, and she paid for it gladly.

"Suppose I tell her who really bought it?" Graham asked Gabby later, when she showed the necklace to him before tucking it into his suitcase.

"You won't."

"Can you be sure?"

Gabby closed the zipper on his valet pack and looked across the loft at him. "Yes. Because you're not a cruel person."

"Only a desperate one."

"Don't be. Be grateful instead."

Gabby saw the muscles work in his face then saw the whole strong face cave in. Graham rushed to her and took her in his arms.

"Without you, I've got nothing," he whispered. His mouth searched hers; his hands were everywhere on her body at once.

"Without you, I am nothing. I was nothing until I met you, and I will be nothing when you are gone. You are what instilled in me the desire to strive for that never-reached goal. With you, I achieved everything you wanted."

Rum Springs
December 29, 1976

The room without her in it was barren and lifeless.
Through the morning chill, I could smell the lingering
scent of her perfume. If the room suffered this much,
how much more would I suffer with Gabby gone?

G raham turned in his sleep and reached for Gabby. He found only empty space and cold sheets.

"Gabby?" He called her name as he sat up in bed. When there was no answer, he got up quickly, pulled on his clothes, then hurried down the stairs. He was terrified.

Outside, the night's snowfall had covered the earth with a fresh cloak of beauty. The air had a dry clarity; the light, a pale brilliance. The world was washed by the pure mountain winds.

Sentinels of firs bent heavy, snow-flecked branches toward the earth. Mountain walls rose a mile high, dotted with timberlines of majestic pines. The purple-dappled shadows of the foothills gave way to blinding light up the mountain, where the rays of the rising sun hit the higher peaks.

Graham was aware of the sound and smell of perking coffee coming from the kitchen. In the living room, the fire burned cheerily. When the coffeemaker gurgled to a stop, Graham poured two mugs of steaming coffee and carried them to the fire; that done, he simply sat down and waited.

At length, Gabby stomped her feet on the deck to shake off the snow then threw the door open.

"Hi," she said.

She wore faded jeans, a bulky white sweater, hiking boots,

and her suede jacket. A long scarf that matched the sweater hung around her neck. She'd left her hair down for Graham.

"You frightened me," Graham told her softly.

Gabby took off her jacket and went to sit beside him at the fire. "I won't leave without saying good-bye," she promised.

"Even if it seems easier at the time?"

Gabby gave him an intense look. "If I wanted easy, I wouldn't be here. I knew love could be so wonderful and yet so unbearably filled with pain," she said simply.

They returned phone calls from the message slips she brought back, then bundled up against the cold and went out the back door. Today, by unspoken agreement, they would avoid the seminar and its participants. Neither of them could withstand a repeat of last night's conversation in the bar.

Struggling along cleared and not-cleared paths, knee-deep in drifts, sheltered by the sweet-smelling branches of waving pines, they climbed up the mountain. At length, they broke through the woods and emerged at a point far above the world.

On a rocky overhang, high above a jagged canyon where the earth dropped away at frightening speeds, they stopped to rest. Far across the valley below, they could see the bright-jacketed skiers on the opposite slopes.

The sun was high in the sky, and it warmed them despite the cold and snow. The sky was intensely blue and winter perfect. Not a sound intruded on the silence, not even the sigh of a breeze or the whisper of a bird's wing in flight.

"We could just stay," Graham said. He looked out over the vista below them. "Cut down a tree, build a cabin. Never go back."

Gabby barely nodded. She was drinking in the quiet beauty and storing it away. "We could," she said. "But we won't."

Graham sighed. It was loud and foreign in the stillness. "Please?"

"The world won't let us, Graham. Sooner or later, it would intrude. Sooner or later, we'd have to face reality. Sooner or later, we'd have to face the people we'd hurt. You're not very fond of the world, are you?"

"Not right now, because going back to the world means leaving you. Trouble is, I can't really find an alternative."

"We could look together."

Gabby shook her head. A ray of winter sunshine cut through the trees and washed her face in light so clear, you could see the future in it.

"The world is all we have. All we're given." Gabby's voice was as soft as the drifted snow.

"No," Graham said. "You and I have more. We have love."

"I think we've only been lent it. Maybe someday we'll even know why."

Graham looked at her closely. Gabby knew her eyes were seeing things far away, things Graham hadn't faced yet.

"You're sad this morning, aren't you?" he asked.

Gabby thought about that as she looked out across the beautiful valley. "Yes," she finally answered. "Not for what I've gained by knowing you. For what I'll have to give up."

"The cost," Graham said quietly, "may end up being more than I can bear."

"Then don't let it be that way."

Rum Springs
Thursday, December 30, 1976

Chalet In Rum Springs

*He saw the sight of her huddled before the fire, so
fragile, so alone. It would be imprinted forever and
ever across his mind and go on through eternity.*

"What are you doing down here?" Graham asked her.
The sky was gradually lightening from soot-washed
pewter to a pearly dawn. It looked like a covey of dusky doves
closely canopied the earth. A few downy flakes still drifted down,
stray feathers from the crouching doves.

"I couldn't sleep," Gabby said. She sat very still in front of the
fire, her knees pulled up under her chin.

"Want coffee?"

"Please. It's already made," she said. Still, she focused on the
fire.

Graham went back, carefully balancing a hot mug in each
hand. He handed her one, then sank down beside her on the
rug.

"You're brooding," he said.

"I'm all right," Gabby whispered.

"No, you aren't," Graham said. "Don't close up on me." He
reached a hand over and touched her cheek.

Gabby closed her eyes and felt the touch of his hand burn its
image into her skin. She knew she'd carry the warmth forever.
She took his hand in hers, brought it to her lips, and kissed his
palm. "I love you so much," she said.

"And I love you." Graham stroked her hair, as if trying to
memorize the play of lights in its golden thickness. He ran a

finger over her cheek, outlining the hollow of her cheekbones, her full mouth, the deep shadow of her lashes in the firelight.

"What would you like to do today?" he asked gently.

"I know what I don't want to do," Gabby said. "I don't want to share today with anybody."

"Then we won't. Anything else?"

Gabby buried her face in Graham's shoulder and clung to him desperately.

"Just be with you," she whispered. "Just be with you."

Gabby floated in a place just out of Graham's grasp and comprehension—a dark place, cold and barren. Its presence drifted around her like smoke. This was their last day. Tomorrow they would fly home. Today she had to put a necessary distance between them if she was ever going to be able to leave him.

"Not yet," Graham whispered, reading her mind again. "Don't leave me yet. We have today. We have tonight. If nothing else."

"So hard." Gabby breathed a sob as the tears began to roll down her face. "So damned hard."

"I know." He held her tightly against his body, and Gabby felt the strong contours of him as easily as she felt her throat close up.

"Hold me, Graham, and just love me," she whispered.

Graham carried Gabby up the stairs and into the big featherbed. Time was suspended, floating above them somewhere. Shadows and lights spun around the room. He loved her gently. Then he started over and loved her desperately with a passion he had never known and knew he never would again.

In the end, he merely held her while they both cried.

They dressed slowly, savoring the time, the touches, the loving.

Gabby led him outside, and they built a snowman on the front deck. She carried pots of fresh snow up, shaping and molding the portly body. Graham watched her earnestness with tears clouding his vision.

Gabby went into the chalet and brought back a carrot for a nose and two dead coals from the fire for eyes. She placed them gently, almost reverently, then stood back.

She unwound the long wool scarf around her neck and tied it on the snowman. "Give me your hat."

"My hat?" Graham reached up, took off the navy watch cap he wore, and handed it to her.

Gabby placed it on the snowman at a jaunty angle. When she turned back to Graham, there were tears in her eyes again.

"That way." Gabby nodded to the snowy figure. "We leave something of ourselves up here. When we have to go."

Graham went to her, wrapped his arms around her, and led her into the chalet.

They sat in front of the fire, drinking hot chocolate and watching the dancing flames while the afternoon slipped quietly away. He held her close, breathing in the fresh scent of the mountain air that was captured in her hair.

After nightfall, they walked into town and had a solitary drink in a small bar.

"I want to reach out and touch everything, feel its form and texture," Gabby explained. "Devour it. Take it back with me."

"It could work," Graham told her softly.

Gabby knew how hard he was trying to find some way to stop this plunge toward the abyss, but it was inevitable. She desperately wished he could find a way, oh, how she wished.

Huge flakes of snow began to fall as they started back to the chalet.

"It's too late." It was all Gabby said. It was enough. She knew Graham knew it as well as she did. He just wasn't as willing to give up.

No solitude could equal the loneliness of the two of them as they passed through the shadowed woods.

Far above them, the stars looked down through an infinite silence onto a silence as intense.

Tennessee
December 30, 1993

Beat wildly, heart of mine. Thrash against the walls of your prison.
It will do you no more good.
Pound your anger; rage at the angels who brought this wonderful
life and love to you. Raise your voice; scream at all the devils
who have caused you this pain. Then clutch it to your breast
and thank all heaven and the god who gave it to you.
Take it with you when you leave; let no
other have one as great as this.

Gabby stole into the bathroom of her studio and stared into the mirror. For the first time, she really saw the lines around her eyes, the silver streaks in the still thick and shiny golden hair, the intense blue of the eyes awash in sadness from tonight's tears. It was a face abandoned by hope. Tonight, for the first time, she saw age in her face and realized that time had passed.

I have so deluded you, my faithful heart, she thought. *Telling you to be still and bide your time. Telling you to be patient. To wait for a tomorrow that never came. Nurturing you through dark winters. Letting you soar on countless cloudless summer days. Listening to you in the rain. Does it help you to know I didn't do it on purpose? Does it help you to know I'm as surprised as you are? Will knowledge ease either of us of our pain?*

Gabby turned away from the mirror and went back to her studio. There, she eased the closet door open. Upstairs, all was silent and still.

From under a clutter of discarded canvases and filled sketch pads, from under boxes she saved for reasons obscure and ribbons she saved to tie the boxes, far back in the corner sat the bag she'd bought on the way to the doctor's office. Careful not to disturb anything, she pulled it out.

Her hands shook as she retrieved the bottle of premixed margaritas. This was the first year she'd thought to toast the date with a margarita. Had something told her this year would be different? This year would be the year she finally, finally, took seriously the fact that she could call USC and get in contact with Graham if she wanted to, and if she decided to, if the hurt and loss were too much to bear alone anymore.

She went to the kitchen, got a glass, filled it with ice, then carried it back to the safety of her sanctuary. She sat cross-legged on the futon and filled the glass to the brim.

She raised the glass and made a toast to herself and the memories of Graham while the tears fell once more from her face.

"To loves unfinished and dreams unlived," she softly toasted. "And to a heart that was never free and will never be free unless it's with you, Graham, my love, my life."

Rum Springs
Friday, December 31, 1976

The snow had now become a steady wall of white, falling from a starless sky. He searched the darkness ahead for Gabby, didn't see her, then started for the chalet. He found her when he got there, sitting on the steps, huddled against the cold and looking forlorn.

Looking up into Graham's eyes, Gabby saw more love than she'd ever seen anywhere. And she didn't know what she could do about it and how to be true to promises made before she met him.

"It wouldn't be bad," he said. "We'd make sure the kids understood."

"Understood what, Graham? That I selfishly left the only father they've ever known for my happiness? You can't explain that to an adult, never mind a child."

"Ah, Gabby, please. We've got to find some way. I can't..."

He didn't finish the sentence. He didn't have to. Gabby knew exactly what he meant.

"Make love to me, Graham," she whispered.

"Ah, God," Graham breathed. He pulled Gabby to her feet.

"Now," she said. "I can't wait, Graham."

Graham drew in a sharp breath, picked Gabby up effortlessly, and carried her into the chalet.

Her eyes never left his as she undressed and stood, proud and ageless, before him. His hand reached for her breasts, and he watched her.

"Hank has the hots for you," he said.

"Hank doesn't get me," Gabby whispered, her hands caressing Graham's body. "You do."

"Ah, Gabby," he said. His mouth closed over hers. His hands pulled the firm body tight against him, and Gabby pressed close to him.

"I love you so much," she whispered. "So much," she repeated.

Gabby's tears were right there again, just beneath the surface. Looking up at Graham, she knew his were too.

What am I supposed to do when this is over? Go home to my life
and convince myself none of it ever happened?
Go home to my wife and pretend none of it was real?
Well, let me tell you, Gabby Franks, it was real,
and for me it will never end. As the poets say, "Even
after death, I shall but love you even more."

"It's only a banquet," Gabby told Graham. She wound a strand of pearls loosely into the thick coil of her hair. She'd put on a striking black sweater dress that was midcalf and elegant. With it she wore a pair of tall black suede boots with stiletto heels. The neckline of the dress was scooped indecently low, and her breasts looked translucent and dusted with diamond powder in the light of the bedroom.

"I just thought we should be seen at least once a day at something. Since we have to eat anyway, why not the banquet?"

"It steals our time," Graham said.

"It broadens the scope of our remembrances," Gabby countered softly. She held a pearl-trimmed cameo on a velvet ribbon around her neck. Graham went over to her and tied it then kissed the warm nape of her neck. His arms went around her, and his hands automatically caressed her warm and soft, responding body.

"I don't want memories," he said huskily. "I want you."

"Then we won't go," Gabby said simply. "We'll fix something downstairs."

Graham took a deep breath as he watched her in the mirror.

"No," he said quietly. "You're right. I want to remember more about you than how you looked in bed." Gabby nodded silently and picked up her ankle-length fur coat.

"Can we go in together?" Graham asked, holding the coat for her.

"Yes. Hank asked me this morning if I planned on attending the meetings today."

"He did?"

"Yes. When I picked up our messages."

"What did you tell him?"

Gabby turned and looked at Graham steadily. "That you and I had other plans for today."

"You did?"

"Yes," she said softly. "I did."

"And?"

Gabby smiled the smile she had for Graham, the smile that was his and his alone. Down through the ages, she'd never smiled it for anyone else, and she knew she never would. "He told me to offer you his congratulations. He also said he hoped we had a wonderful day. He also said if either of us got any emergency messages, he'd bring them over." Gabby smiled. "Knock twice then leave them stuck in the door."

"You do make good friends, don't you?"

"It's all give-and-take." Gabby started down the stairs with Graham close behind.

"He's met Patti, you know." Graham pulled his topcoat on over his dark suit

"That has no relevance to us, Graham—not here, not now. If we don't give it relevance, neither will Hank."

Graham pulled the door closed behind them and took Gabby's arm. The moon was a silver pendant against a velvet backdrop. It washed the snow with cold, pale light. Overhead, the light of a million stars looked down on them. The snow formed strange and wondrous shapes, secret places, drifts of dark promise among the swaying shadows.

"Do we have to stay long?" Graham asked.

Gabby was smiling again when she answered. "Hardly any time at all."

They'd almost missed the cocktail hour completely. Hank spied them as they went in. He waved and started toward them as Graham took their coats to the cloakroom and detoured past the bar.

Hank shot back his crisp and spotless white cuff and looked at his watch. "Running a little late?"

"Couldn't decide what to wear," Gabby said easily. "You know women. They change clothes a dozen times."

"Uh-huh." Hank grinned. "Well, you made an excellent choice."

"Thank you."

Graham came up and handed Gabby a glass of white wine. She sipped it delicately while she looked around the elegant room.

"No toast?" Hank raised an eyebrow.

Gabby looked at him with a steady gaze. "To brief interludes," she said as she raised her glass. "May they be remembered by those involved and forgotten by those not."

Hank inclined his head while the ghost of a smile lit his face. "Done," he assured her.

On the way back, through the endless starry night, Graham looked down at Gabby. "Brief interlude?" he asked. "Is that how you see this?"

Gabby replied, "It's how I wanted Hank to see it."

"But not how you see it?". Graham asked.

Rum Springs Ski Resort

As they neared the entrance to the chalet, Gabby stopped and turned to Graham. Both hands were deep in her pockets, and she knew she'd retreated to the place where Graham didn't have the nerve to follow her yet.

"Everything you start can't be forever, Graham," she said. "I didn't make the rules. I just try to live by them. And the rules tell me that when the world moves on, we have to as well."

"I don't want to move on," Graham told her. "I can't go on—no, Gabby, I can't go back to my old life and forget about this. I'm not going back to my old life at all if you give me a choice."

Gabby stared sightlessly up at the heavens. The world was held captive in a sudden and unexpected hush. A stray breeze, coming from nowhere and going nowhere, rippled past her.

"Do we have a place in the real world, Graham?" Gabby asked. Her voice was a whisper in the dark. "Together? When we've already made other choices? Made promises to other people? Isn't that the reality, Graham? The lives we left behind. The commitments we made before we found each other. How can we not go back to that?"

Gabby's heart almost broke when she looked back at Graham and saw the tears in his eyes, the loss written so plainly over his face. *God, how can it hurt so much,* she wondered, *and still be the right thing to do?* The two stood still as statues, frozen in space. Somewhere in the distance, a nightbird cried. Just once, then it was silent. Overhead, the cold moon peered over the tops of the trees. Blue shadows were on the falling white snow. The scent of the pines was a perfume to her. It was something she would always remember.

Graham looked down at Gabby standing so still and so quiet beside him. She could tell he was afraid to reach out for her, afraid she would disappear at his human touch. His fear was nothing compared to hers.

"You're not going to give me a choice, are you, Gabby?" Graham asked.

Gabby could feel him holding his breath as he waited for the eternity that passed before she finally answered him. The brooding night closed in on them both, and the moonlight lit the tears on the face Gabby turned up to Graham. Her golden hair had turned moon-washed silver and matched her tears.

"I don't think I can," she whispered. "Don't you see? It would destroy us all."

Back at the chalet, Graham hung up their coats then took Gabby by the hand and led her to the fire. She stood, silent and watchful, as he slid the dress off her shoulders and let it fall to the floor. Her tears were dry on her cheeks, but in the endless depths of her eyes was the promise of more.

"Don't cry," Graham whispered. "Please. It breaks my heart."

"I love you," Gabby whispered. "And I didn't expect it to be this hard. I didn't know love could ever or would ever hurt this much."

Graham undressed while Gabby's eyes caressed him, loved him, yearned for him; she took his very shape and being into her soul and locked it there for eternity.

Graham took her hand and pulled her down in front of the fire. He leaned on one elbow and traced the delicate contours of her face. Slowly he unwound the coil of heavy hair and let it stream through his fingers. It caught the prisms of firelight and turned a dozen shades of gold, each brighter than the light of a thousand suns.

He kissed her, and Gabby felt the familiar contours of his body press against her. Gently he lay her down. Just as gently he held her in his arms and tenderly gave her the love that had been missing so badly from both of their lives. Tomorrow it would have to be just a memory and stay forever that way.

His warmth filled Gabby completely. Softly at first, then with increasing passion, she arched toward him, need meeting need. She was lost inside herself—all feeling, no thought.

It was as if Graham were weightless against her pinned body.

He floated endlessly over her until their world exploded in a shower of lights and stars.

The sweet scent of their love blended with the woodsmoke and her soft perfume. Slowly the world quit spinning, and the room regained its soft focus.

Gabby reached up and brushed Graham's face. "You've stolen my heart, stolen my soul, stolen my body. And when this is over, you'll steal my happiness, if not my life."

"Don't let the evil trolls take this away from us," Graham whispered. "Fight them. Don't give up, Gabby."

"Oh god, Graham," Gabby said. "I want to. Can't you see that? I wish I could will the evil trolls away. Be born again tomorrow, with no past and no history. Be born again just for you."

She sat up and moved away. Her tears were sudden, swift rivers running down her cheeks. She stared into the flickering blue flames while Graham's hands softly caressed her hair. He gathered her in his arms, and his lips were soft and searching in her scented hair.

"Please," he whispered. "Do it. I know we promised not to hurt innocent people, but I can't lose you."

"What are we supposed to do?" The tears were painting tracks down Gabby's cheeks.

"We'll go back, talk to Theo, talk to Patti. Try to explain things to them. Make a life together."

"And the children?"

"We'll make it right for them. I don't know how, but we will. I promise."

Without warning, Gabby's slow tears turned to sobs. They were heartbreaking sobs that shook her fragile body and ripped her soul apart.

"Don't ask me to do that. Because I can't tear other people's lives apart. I don't know how." Gabby's speech was slurred and desperate.

Graham held her as close as he could while he stroked her

head and tried to soothe the frightening sobs. "Everything's changed since this started," he said. "I want to share the rest of my life with you. This isn't enough."

"It's all I have, Graham," Gabby whispered around her tears. "Don't you see it's all we have—it's all we ever had. It has to end."

"Are you going back and close yourself up in a glass cage, Gabby? Insulate yourself from what we're feeling here? Stay in that cage of business aloof, alone, and apart? Do you honestly think that will make this go away?"

"It has to."

"Why? Because you say so?"

"No. Because decency says so, because my children say so."

"We'll take them with us. God, I'd never expect you to leave your children. I'll love them and take care of them like they were my own. You know that."

"We'd kill Theo. He didn't ask for this."

"This will kill us," Graham pleaded. "Which would you rather do?"

"Theo has no part in this, no idea it's even happening. I did it, Graham. If someone has to pay, shouldn't it be me? Not Theo and the children, not Patti."

Graham held her until their bodies blended into one entity in the flickering flames of the fire.

Outside, the wind picked up and vented itself against the night. Large flakes began to fall through a sky suddenly starless and empty. The moon hid behind impatient clouds.

The two lovers' souls were as alone as the overcast sky—dark, void, and empty of life and color.

Tennessee
December 30, 1993

At length, we had to face the truth.
We were no match for the evil trolls.

Icy fingers played a tap dance up Gabby's spine as she sipped from the frosty glass of margaritas. "Damned if we did, damned if we didn't," she repeated softly.

In the end, of course, she was the one to pay. And the price was frightfully high. She'd accepted it for seventeen years. Or so she thought. It wasn't until tonight she realized she'd merely lived with it. It was until tonight she realized a part of her had never accepted it at all. She drew in a deep breath and leaned her head back. Her hands held the aged sketch and fingered its curling edges.

Gabby had gone back to Theo as if nothing had happened. She bottled her grief up. Eventually she assigned it a time and place to come out so she could toy with it, worry it, wallow in it, then put it back. The rest of the time, she managed to keep it in its dark and secret place, an unacceptable intrusion in her busy life.

Jack had opened endless stores across the country. Gabby always helped. The hardest times to stay in control were when she was separated from Theo and the children.

Once, when they were in the southern tip of Florida, Jack asked her to clean up a store in the northern corner of the state. Hire new managers, train them, turn a profit. Order out of chaos, Gabby described it. Jack told her that's why he sent her to do it.

For eight months, she lived in an apartment in a strange town while her youngest went through senior year without her. The store turned out fine. So did her youngest. In fact, he found it glamorous and exciting, having a mother to visit in an elegant apartment in a faraway town. It set him apart from the rest of his friends. Sometimes, she thought Theo liked it for much the same reasons.

During that time, Gabby fought her demons continually. There was always the late-night urge to call California and to try to find Graham so she could fill the emptiness. It was accompanied by the reckless longing to throw everything she had away for one more night of loving him.

She never made the call. Not then, and not when she was in Atlanta, alone again, opening another store for almost a year before Theo was transferred up there.

Gabby stared hard at the phone on her desk. *Can you do it, Gabby?* she asked herself. *Can you make the call that lets you hear Graham's sweet voice again? And lets you see his face? After all this time, are you finally ready to follow your heart, even if all you get is one more night of loving him?*

Outside, she heard the wind whipping around the house. The snow still fell in the glow of the streetlights and blended with the patchy fog. The night raced relentlessly toward midnight.

Tennessee
December 30, 1993

The winter winds blow, and I miss him. The grass grows green with spring, and I miss him. The days turn to lazy mauve softness in summer, and I miss him. The leaves paint the world scarlet with fall, and I miss him. I sleep the restless sleep of love remembered. But I only grieve for him one night a year. My soul can take no more.

Gabby watched the clock on her desk. Watched it move from ten to eleven to... the time was approaching. She always ended her vigils at midnight. After all, it was no longer December 30 after midnight. No longer the last day of their time together.

Her glass was empty. Funny, she barely remembered touching it. Gabby reached over and refilled it, carefully tucked the bottle back in the bag and hid it in her closet, then got up and went to the kitchen for more ice. The annual drink finished and over, she stood at the kitchen window and watched the snowfall.

Tennessee in winter, she thought. *What a place to be.* It was the one and only blatant request Theo ever made of her. Most of the time, when Gabby was faced with a decision, she talked it out with Theo. He gave her his ideas, discussed pros and cons, made her discuss them, then told her to make up her own mind. She was a rational adult.

"If I had you believing that all these years, Theo, I was very good, indeed," Gabby whispered into the silent kitchen.

When Theo was forced into the move to Tennessee, Jack countered with a plan for Gabby. He was opening a new store in Denver. Would she go?

Gabby
Franks

She and Theo handled it as always. They talked about it and weighed the options. Then Theo left her alone to make her decision.

Almost a week later, over a little too much brandy, Theo stepped completely out of character.

"I'm afraid," he said.

"Of what?"

"It's getting too easy."

"What is?" Gabby had asked.

"Being apart. Leading separate lives. It's harder to get back together again each time."

Gabby considered his words, sitting in Atlanta with the photo album open across her knees. She and Theo had sailed the West Indies in October. Visited Saint Bart's, Saint Kitts, Saba, and Nevis. The pictures were back, and she was putting them in the album.

"What are you saying, Theo?"

"I think we're getting too used to being apart. Too used to being alone. I don't want it to become something we can't get back from!"

Gabby studied him in the quiet of the room. She was surprised to see his receding hairline and heavy glasses. With a start, she realized age was catching up with both of them.

"What are you asking me, Theo?" Gabby said quietly.

Theo took a deep breath. Never once had he imposed his will on Gabby, at least knowingly. It cost him. "Move to Tennessee with me," he said softly, finally looking at her.

Gabby saw fear in Theo's eyes. Fear of growing old and doing it alone.

"All right," she said.

Gabby resigned the next day.

Jack went on a three-day drunk.

What would Theo do if I left him now? Would the fear I saw in his eyes in Atlanta destroy him? Or would it still destroy me?

Tennessee
December 30, 1993

*The last ember died in the fire, and we let it lie dead
and empty on the cold hearth. Like our hearts.*

Gabby went back to her studio and picked up the watercolor sketch. "One more night by the fire, Graham," she whispered. "While I think about my options." She went silently through the familiar house to the living room, carrying the sketch. The fire was dying. She added a small log, stoked it back to life, and then sat across it. She stared into the fire, remembering the first day she went back to work after Rum Springs.

Jack took one worried, concerned look at her face and asked her what the hell happened to her.

She smiled sadly. Smiled through the ages for all the pain and loss and despair that passed through the world from creation to the present.

"I flew too close to the flames" was all she said.

Rum Springs
Friday, December 30, 1976

A giant hand closed around her heart, holding
it, squeezing it, until it was dead.

Gabby propped herself up on her elbow and watched Graham stir beside her. He reached for her automatically.

Will he do that when he gets home? she wondered.

Graham opened his eyes and looked at her with infinite sadness. They'd made love all night, barely sleeping for an hour.

"It's time," Gabby said softly.

"No." It was a choked cry, wrenched from the depths of Graham's soul.

"I met you, and I loved you," Gabby said simply. "Now I have to let you go. I have to give you back."

The truth in her words didn't make the burden easier for either of them. Pain swirled around them, palpable and pulsing.

Graham reached over and took her in his arms. He held her as tightly as he could.

In her heart, Gabby knew this would be the last time he would hold her like this or she would hold him.

"I'll always love you. Nothing can take that away from me," Graham whispered.

Slowly they dressed and packed luggage reluctantly. They started down the stairs for the last time. Loss, love, and bittersweet memories haunted every step of their progress and shadowed their footsteps.

It was a dreadful preview of what their tomorrows would be.

The snowman stood staunchly on the deck, cap at its jaunty angle and scarf blowing in the wind. Graham locked the door behind them for the final time.

Gabby rested her head on his shoulder on the plane back to Boise, still and silent, facing her future.

When they landed, Graham left the plane before she did. Theo was meeting her, after all.

Gabby waited on the plane so long after Graham left that the stewardess asked her if she was all right.

"I have to be," Gabby told her. "I have no choice."

With the girl watching her suspiciously, Gabby gathered up the strength to walk down the aisle of the small plane and out into the waiting area.

Theo waited by the door. He looked terribly glad to see her.

Behind Theo, Gabby saw Graham. He stood in the shadows and watched them.

Gabby knew in that instant, as Theo planted a kiss on her cheek, what a heart felt like when it broke.

On the lower level, while they waited for their baggage, Graham met Gabby's eyes across the crowd. He stood very still, eyes locked with hers.

The two lovers were alone in the crowded airport, alone in time past and time forward. They both felt the aged spirits gather around them. Spirits that rose from the glacier-washed earth one final time, walked across the bones of the dinosaurs, chased the mastodons, and lit the fires.

A swirling mist circled Gabby and Graham as they felt the ancient ones around them—felt them circle, chant, and dance with the moon. Each drum echoed in their breaking hearts.

For the last time, they took one last look toward each other. Then they turned and walked into the old life, knowing there would never be a time or a love as had been between them.

As Theo touched Gabby's arm and she turned to leave, the ancient ones were gone too. They disappeared in a puff of smoke from man's first fire.

"At the moment of our death, will the other one know?"

Patti looked up from the TV. A stifled cry from the living room had disturbed her concentration. "Damn," she muttered. It was just after nine o'clock in California, and one of her favorite shows was playing on the TV set across the den. Never managing to break into show business, Patti passed her time watching the people who had.

She got up and padded through the house. Thank heaven there were no children's toys to form an obstacle course. Neither teenage clothes nor pizza boxes were strewn about. It was a solitary house for just two people. It had been that way since the trip Graham had taken years ago.

"Why the hell Graham has to drink until he passes out this one night a year, I'll never understand. Why can't he wait until New Year's Eve like everyone else?" Patti muttered. "But no. He won't even go out on New Year's Eve."

I never felt the spirits sing again. Never heard the falling water. And I never saw a dinosaur.

Gabby watched the gold watch on her wrist creep up to midnight. Her tears were coursing down her cheeks as she played through her memories again from start to finish. Sitting there, in front of the fire, she acknowledged the dream was dead unless she was brave enough to try and get it back. *Am I? Haven't Graham and I suffered enough? Given enough? Isn't it, finally, our time?*

She heard the clock ticking in the hall, heard the wind blow around the eaves, and heard the wicker furniture on the porch tossed about like furniture in a child's dollhouse. Upstairs, Theo slept the sleep of the unknowing.

For a long time, Gabby simply stared unseeing into the fire.

Finally, she drew in a deep breath and looked around the familiar room.

I'm sorry, Theo, Gabby silently said, *so sorry, but I can't make your world right anymore. My heart won't let me. I have to make mine right now. It's time.*

Gabby kissed her fingertips then placed the fingers tenderly on Graham's sketch. There was no reason to get careless now and leave the sketch someplace it didn't belong.

Slowly, Gabby stood up to take the sketch back to her studio and put it in its hiding place. The first pain hit her the minute she was on her feet. She gasped and tried to sit back down. The doctor's words were a frightening echo booming in her head.

She couldn't make it back to the chair. Her knees buckled under her, and Gabby crumpled to the floor. Heat and lightning traveled through her chest and down her useless left arm. Her heart raced out of control.

Gabby knew at last where the mastodons had gone. They sat, unflinching and unmoving, on her battered chest. Darkness crept around her, wavering, rippling. She still clasped Graham's sketch in her hand.

"No," she whispered. Tears of pain and regret washed down her cheeks. *So close,* she thought. *So close again, oh, my love. I'm sorry, Graham, so sorry. We waited too long.*

Gabby tried to still her heart, to will the pains away. It was no use, and she knew it.

With the last of her strength, Gabby pulled herself across the floor to the fire. Marshaling her movements to coincide with the pounding of her heart and the pulsing pain, she managed to push the aged sketch into the flames.

She watched with the last of her earthly vision as the edges crumpled and burned, watched until the fire consumed the sketch. As she lay there, the firelight caught the glint of polished and old pearl earrings under her golden hair.

"Ashes to ashes. Dust unto dust."

Theo found Gabby the next morning when Annie's soulful howls woke him. After he'd gone through the formalities, after the doctor examined Gabby and the men came for her body, Theo notified the children.

Then he sat down and pondered the place on the floor where Gabby died. Briefly, he wondered why she never told him about her heart. Not that it mattered now.

In the years to come, when he thought about her, and he thought about her often, two things would always puzzle Theo.

Why did she have a smile of such peace and homecoming on her face when she died? It was a smile Theo had never seen her smile before.

And why did she die arm outstretched and so close to the flames?

Graham sat in the recliner by the fire. A half-empty bottle of Jack Daniel's was on the table beside him, along with a heavy glass. One hand rested on the center of his chest. There was something wrong; there was an emptiness he felt.

"Graham? Are you all right?" Patti said as she flicked on a lamp. "What is it now?"

Graham was pale and distracted. "Nothing. I fell asleep and had a bad dream. Go on back to your show."

Patti frowned. "Passed out is more like it," she muttered. She turned the lamp off and headed back to the den and her TV set.

Only moments earlier, Graham had felt Gabby in the room with him. Sensed her presence, saw her smile, felt her hand touch his, then he had smelled her fragrance.

The winds blew, and he heard the ancients chant again. He

felt the winds swirl. He smelled the smoke of distant fires, heard falling waters.

Now, he sat silently in the dark with the fire while tears slid down his cheeks. Gabby was gone. He knew it as certainly as he would know his own death when it came.

It was now seventeen years later, on the anniversary of their parting, and Gabby was gone.

The dream was dead.

He'd never see the spirits dance again.

—The End—

Graham, if you are out there, please let me know. I have a message for you from your Gabby.